THE WORLD OF RHYTHM CALLED RITUALS

Rituals mean any stylised behaviour that recurs, they abound in all walks of life, and in rituals manifest rhythms, subtle or loud.

The World of Rhythm Called Rituals

JAYANT BURDE

New Age Books

ISBN: 978-81-7822-332-2
First Edition: Delhi, 2009

Published by
NEW AGE BOOKS
A-44 Naraina Phase-I
New Delhi–110 028(INDIA)
Email: nab@vsnl.in
Website: www.newagebooksindia.com

Printed in India
at Shri Jainendra Press
A-45 Naraina Phase–I, New Delhi–110 028

DEDICATION

I dedicate this book to those authors who have immensely influenced me and whose works have proved to be rich sources for my own writings though I have often disagreed with their views. The most important among them are:

Ayn Rand
Bertrand Russell
Deepak Chopra
Fritjof Capra
Frits Staal
Pandit Rajamani Tigunait
Sigmund Freud

Contents

Preface

This book explains how rituals are closely connected with verse, music and dance. It asserts that like music and dance rituals belong to the world of rhythm. By *ritual* we mean any stylised behaviour that recurs. Rituals abound in all walks of life: social intercourse, military affairs, law and politics, education and so forth. In most rituals rhythm is manifest and loud. In a few rituals which have a slow tempo; some analysis is necessary to detect rhythmic patterns.

The book is written for the common reader. I have avoided diacritical marks, mathematical and logical symbols and many technical devices which were used in my earlier book. *Rituals, Mantras and Science: An Integral Perspective (2004)*. The main purpose of writing that book was to show that there can be a science of rituals and I heavily borrowed from Frits Staal's work *Rituals and Mantras: Rules without Meaning*. In the present book my main goal is to show that like music and dance, rituals belong to the world of rhythm. I have also discussed at greater length the *ritual instinct* which was conceptualised in the earlier book.

The notes which I have added after each chapter are meant for those who would like to know more about the relevant topic. The reader who feels that notes are unnecessary hurdles which merely impede reading may totally ignore them.

There are many technical words from music, dance and religion. These have been explained in the text. Nevertheless I have provided a glossary which can be used for ready reference.

Jayant Burde

Acknowledgments

While the Author's name appears prominently below the title of the book, the contribution of many others, though hidden, is equally important. I have already mentioned Dr. Frits Staal to whom I am indebted. I thank Mr. Rajiv Jain, Ms. Jyotsna and the staff of New Age Books for speedy completion of editing and preparing the CRC. Needless to say I am thankful to my relatives and friends who helped me in many ways. Of course, my thanks also go to Mr. Yashwant Dusane who prepared the computer-aided script.

Jayant Burde

Introduction

Have you seen a two-month old baby perform a rhythmic exercise in which it rotates its hands and legs? Doctors rightly call this ritual activity 'cycling'. As it grows the baby displays more and more such rhythmic behaviour. For example, its babbling such as

ba ba ba ba
pa pa pa pa
ma ma ma ma
va va va va
ai ai ai ai

is full of rhythm.

Human adults, too, display ritualistic behaviour either consciously or unconsciously. They hum a tune when they are elated, pace up and down when they are anxious and make rhythmic sounds when they are playing with children. Animals, too, engage in ritualistic behaviour. Higher primates such as chimpanzees experiment with different sounds by repeated banging and striking. Other members of their society may join them and enjoy the percussion. Many animals make repetitive vocal sounds, such as hoots and screams in which an individual may soon be joined by the entire group. Animals, too, respond to music rhythmically by swaying as human adults and babies do. They also perform what are called animal rituals such as aspersion rites or combat rituals (in which they have no real intention to engage in fight).

In most of the ritualistic behaviour mentioned above, rhythm is quite patent. It would not be wrong to say that wherever there is ritual, there is rhythm. The second aspect of rituals mentioned above is that neither human babies nor animals have to be taught rhythmic rituals. These rituals appear automatically under proper conditions. We may safely assume that this innate capacity is due to what may be called the *ritual instinct* or rhythm instinct. Even in case of rituals performed by human adults, the ritual instinct plays a dominant role, but in this case instinct is tempered by cultural factors as we shall see later.

You must remember that in this book the word 'ritual' is used in a broad sense to indicate any stylised and recurring behaviour. It is not used in a restricted sense merely to refer to rigid rituals, especially those found in religion. Incidentally rituals can be rigid (formal) or flexible (informal), long or short, simple or complex.

Rituals appear in all walks of life: social intercourse (greeting, manners), religion (worship, rites of passage such as marriage), politics and law (elections, enactment of laws, parliamentary procedure), military affairs (parade, dress, ranks, treatment of war prisoners), education (lectures, conduct of examinations), recreation (sports and games, music and dance).

But what is rhythm? We *feel* rhythm when we hear music, see a dance, listen to drum beats, watch soldiers parading or listen to a priest chanting mantras. In fact our own reaction to ritual rhythm is also rhythmic. When we hear music, we may start humming, tapping, clapping or swaying. Broadly speaking repetition in time or space especially with regularity characterises rhythm.

If we analyse rituals in general we find that there are 10-12 patterns of which repetition, refrain, palindrome and chorus are found in almost all rituals. Other patterns such as relay, overlapping, multiplets, pattern completion, embedding, cycle etc. appear with varying frequencies depending on the type of ritual. We shall call these patterns *ritual patterns* or *ritual structures.*

In *repetition*, the same ritual element appears successively. In the baby's babbling mentioned above, *ba* is repeated in the first line, *pa* in the second line and so forth. *Refrain* is a ritual element which appears periodically. If a devotee chants "Rama, Rama, ..." and prostrates before an idol after every ten utterings, his prostrations are refrains while every block contains ten repetitions of *Ramas. Palindrome* or *mirror* is a pattern in which a part of the sequence of ritual elements appears as a mirror image of the other part. Thus in a simple prayer *Om namah Shivaya* (Hail to Lord Shiva) is often extended as

Om namah Shivaya, Shivaya namah Om.

The second part 'Shivaya namah Om' is an image of the first part 'Om namah Shivaya'. This is equivalent to saying that the ritual appears the same from the beginning to the end as from the end to the beginning.

The word *chorus,* is borrowed from music. When many people perform the same ritual simultaneously, you have an instance of chorus in ritual. The baby's 'cycling' provides an example of the ritual pattern called *cycle.*

Most of the ritual patterns also appear in verse, music, percussion and dance with which we associate rhythm. This aspect should make us wonder whether rhythm is simply a regular repetition in time or space, or something more complex: a bundle of ritual patterns. So closely related are rhythm (symbolised by verse, music and dance) and ritual that we can use the idiom of ritual in rhythm and *vice versa.* For example, the word relay borrowed from sports can be used in music and the word refrain from verse can be applied to ritual.

Analysis of rituals based on structure is called the syntactic (relating to syntax) approach to rituals. A better known approach is concerned with the meaning of ritual.

However, meaning cannot be easily discerned especially in case of traditional rituals which originated centuries ago. For many reasons which are discussed later, rituals are distorted as time passes. The net result is that there can be scores of interpretations, some of them diametrically opposite to others. This has led some scholars like Staal to conclude that some Vedic rituals such as shrauta rituals are meaningless.

The structural approach has opened a new dimension in the study of rituals. The fact that music and dance display almost all ritual patterns convinces us that rituals constitute a world of rhythm.

1

What is Ritual?

When someone mentions rituals we usually think of *religious rituals* such as prayer, puja, marriage ceremonies, sermons and so on. However, if we introspect a little, we realise that we spend most of our life in performing rituals of one type or another. If you recall your activities on a typical working day you will find it difficult to remember an interval of time when you are not ritualising. Most of your activities from morning till night are ritualistic. Getting up, bathing, having breakfast, reading news paper, going to office, having a lunch break, returning home, watching TV and then going to bed; they all constitute a sequence of rituals. Even at night you are performing, albeit unconsciously, such rituals as sleeping, dreaming, snoring and so forth.

Stylised Behaviour

Of course, we are using the word 'ritual' in a very broad sense to connote a stylised and repetitive behaviour. We also call it *stereotyped behaviour* though there may be a few variations. For example, on a certain day you may lunch with your boss while on the next day you may entertain your clients in a restaurant.

If we tend to associate rituals with religion, it is because in olden days religion was much more important than it is today. What's more, religious rituals were solemn, rigid and sometimes very long. There was not only solemnity but also awe, fear and some element of compulsion associated with them. The word 'ritual' is closely related to another word 'rite' which comes from Latin *ritus* (religious usage).

While all of us perform rituals throughout the day, some rituals are common while others belong to specific fields with which individuals are closely associated. Some of these areas where rituals are prominent may be mentioned.

Social life: manners and etiquettes, customs, folkways and mores relating to greeting, conversing, eating, bathing, excreting, courtship, dress code; rites of 'internsification' which make a social group stronger.

Religion: rites of passage, *i.e.*, the rites which mark a new stage in a person's life; the 'last rites' or burial and cremation rites; modes and rules relating to worship; conduct of religious institutions, code of conduct for priests and other officials of temples, churches etc.

Politics and law: rules relating to elections, government formation, legislative and parliamentary procedure, enactment of laws, the law of nations *i.e.*, the public international law, private international law, international protocol and so on.

Defence: parade, rules relating to behaviour among different ranks, war games, code of conduct especially rules regarding secrecy and allegiance, rules relating to war and war prisoners.

Education: rules regarding the establishment and governance of educational institutions, code of conduct for students, teachers and administrative officials, conduct of examinations, and award of diplomas and degrees.

Recreation: music, dancing, gymnastics, sports, cinema, plays; rules pertaining to establishment of clubs and other institutions relating to recreation.

Types of Rituals

There are many criteria on the basis of which rituals may be classified.

Rituals may be *simple* or *complex.* Suppose you are attending a function with your friend Sameer. You bump into a person who happens to be Sameer's friend. Sameer introduces you to him. You may say 'Hello' or 'namaste', and he replies with similar words of greeting. Sameer talks to him for about two minutes and then you part. You may never meet Sameer's friend again in your life. This is an example of a simple ritual.

On the other hand, certain religious rituals tend to be complex in which scores of different types of ritual elements may be present; chanting of mantras, addressing various deities, offering each deity his or her favourite flowers and sweets and so forth.

Rituals may also be classified as *long* and *short.* A long ritual need not be complex and a short ritual may have a higher degree of complexity. For example: the President of your nation may appear on TV and greet you on the occasion of the Republic Day followed by a short speech. This ritual actually involves millions of TV viewers, but the greetings are nevertheless simple because all the viewers are passive and have no option but to listen to the President. Similarly when a foreign dignitary visits your country he may be introduced to a number of people standing in line. This protocol may last for half an hour, and involve many handshakes. Nevertheless, it is a simple ritual. It may be a little more complex than the President's address because the people who are in the queue for greeting the dignitary usually stand in order of 'precedence' determined by the international custom. Complexity of a ritual depends on the structure of the whole ritual; the number of ritual elements, variety of ritual acts and the number of interconnections between the *actors* or ritualists and other ritual elements.

Some rituals are informal *i.e.,* allow considerable flexibility. When you meet a close friend after many years, both of you are excited. There may be an exchange of greetings; you may talk about your families and common friends, but both of you have many options in which you can express your feelings or convey information. In a *formal* ritual there is a great deal of rigidity. For instance, when the elected members of Parliament are administered an oath of office and secrecy, they have to follow the exact rules and use the prescribed linguistic expressions for oath-taking.

You must have realised that we follow rigid or formal rituals on solemn occasions while flexibility appears in social intercourse when the atmosphere is informal. However, a rigid ritual need not be long or complex. Conversely, an informal ritual need not be short. For example, a religious head may bless you with a single gesture of touching your head, an act which is simple as well as short. An informal gathering, on the other hand, may last for two or three hours and become complex because the number of interconnections between the actors, and the topics may tend to increase as time passes.

The following illustrations will give you an idea about how ritual may be judged on these three scales: simple-complex, short-long, flexible-rigid; the last scale may also be called informal-formal.

(1) In Hinduism the word 'Om' or 'Aum' is considered the most sacred mantra. Its repetition alone is believed to bestow upon you material as well as spiritual benefits. Suppose you decide to chant this mantra 10,000 times in one session.

The Sequence

Om, Om, Om, ...

constitutes a ritual which is simple, long and formal. Its degree of rigidity can be increased if your guru (spiritual teacher) insists that this monosyllable must be pronounced in a particular manner with the right intonation.

(2) Suppose you repeat another well-known mantra

Om namah Shivaya (Hail to Lord Shiva)

twenty times in one sitting. The ritual is short, simple though more complex than the previous one, and formal.

(3) You go for your usual morning walk. You accidentally meet your neighbour with whom you have only a slight acquaintance.

You: Good morning.

He: Hello, nice weather.

The ritual is simple, informal and short.

(4) Finance minister introduces his budget proposal in Parliament. He speaks for about three hours and his speech is laced with humour, quotations from Shakespear, and a few maxims from scriptures. The ritual is long. Though formal, it is less rigid than oath-taking mentioned earlier. It is complex but not of a very high degree because though the proposal may involve various topics and statistics: it is not a debate; and the other members do not actively participate in the process.

(5) Basically there are two types of Vedic rituals; *shrauta* and *grihya.* The former are complex and are also called 'traditional' or 'public' ritual. The latter are domestic rituals performed in connection with birth, marriage, etc. which mark the transition in life stages.

Shrauta rituals are usually dedicated to Agni (fire) and Soma, a plant from which a hallucinogenic drink was extracted. Both, Agni and Soma were treated as gods.

Agnichayana is a complex shrauta ritual. Literally the word means 'piling of Agni'. It lasts for twelve days and continues even at some nights during this period. Hence, it is also called *Atiratra* ('overnight'). It involves many priests, *yajamana* on whose behalf the ritual is performed and his wife. It incorporates many sub-rituals of offerings, sacrifices, recitation and chanting of Vedic mantras, extraction of Soma juice, ritual baths, transport of Agni (fire) and so on. All rites are to be performed as prescribed in *Shrauta Sutras,* those manuals composed between eighth and fourth century BCE. This ritual is long, complex and very rigid. It is almost extinct but still survives in a few pockets of Kerala, an Indian State.

In fact shrauta rituals consist of a *hierarchy* of rites. According to Staal they incorporate four basic rituals involving oblation of milk, rice and barley, one ritual involving animal sacrifice, seven types of Soma rituals, and finally Agnichayana which is at the apex of the hierarchy. Agnichayana involves most other shrauta rituals which may recur in the interval of twelve days of this grand ritual, Atiratra.[1]

To understand how a ritual differs from a non-ritual in rigidity suppose in the worship of a certain deity, flowers called 'red flowers' are to be offered. This is a rare flower which grows only in your village and another town A, 1000 kilometers away from your village. Tradition requires that you have to get the flowers from the town A. A botanist tells you that the flower in your village is no different from that grown in town A. The rigid rules require that the flowers from the town A are sacred and for a particular ceremony they cannot be substituted. Despite the easy availability of this flower, you have to travel to town A and bring the sacred flowers. A rigid ritual cannot allow you to deviate from the prescribed rules, although you may attain the same goal by using an alternate method.

Of the three scales mentioned above which is the most important measure that characterises ritual? The answer is 'rigidity'. In fact it is rigidity and repetition which makes our behaviour ritualistic. Even in informal rituals, actors have limited options of behaviour. Suppose you bump into a close friend on a street and say 'Hi'. In reply he gives you a heavy blow on the head with a hockey stick he is carrying. I leave it to you to decide whether you will call this episode a ritual.

This illustration incidentally explains why we use rituals in social life. Rituals make social intercourse easier. We know exactly how we should behave in a given situation. One who is properly socialised behaves almost automatically under various circumstances. To a great extent our world becomes predictable; there are fewer 'shocks' and we feel more secure.

End Note

[1] You can find more about Agnichayana ritual in Staal (1993), chapter 8.

2

Rhythm in Rituals

Broadly there are two methods of studying rituals. The first method pertains to the meaning of ritual and is known as the *semantic* analysis. This approach is also more widely used than the second method which has originated only recently. The latter examines the structure of rituals relegating the *semantic* approach to a less important position.

You may wonder why structure rather than meaning should be given more importance. The reason is that while some rituals can be easily understood, others appear weird and even meaningless.

Meaning and Structure

Suppose you see a devotee prostrating before an idol of a god. His prayer is brief: "O God, save my child from this terrible disease, I beseech you." He also touches the ground with his forehead three times. The meaning of this ritual is fairly clear, though you may not understand which ailment has afflicted his child.

Consider now another case where you find a holy man utter the following words:

Om yam yim yum yaum yah om a vayavya ya vayavyo ma
Vayavya va vayavya.
Yo vayavya cha vayavya ya vayavyo.

The incantations are interspersed with a few gestures by the man. In all probability you will not understand either these words or the gestures although you may have studied

Sanskrit. To you this is a meaningless ritual, but the holy man himself might explain to you the meaning of the prayer. Unfortunately you find several interpretations of a given ritual. This is why the scholars have thought of another approach: they analyse the sturctures of different rituals and try to find out if there are some definite patterns which characterise rituals in general, and also if rituals pertaining to a certain field say, religion, have identifiable peculiarities. Borrowing the terminology from grammar the structural approach is also called the *syntactic* approach.

Consider another simple ritual. A devotee stands with folded hands in which the palms of both hands touch each other and are close to the chest. This is a usual posture of praying in Hinduism and Buddhism. It also seems to have prevailed among early Christians and you still find it as a formal posture among the Church priests on certain occasions. Incidentally, this posture is also used in India and South East Asia for showing respect and in greeting.

Now suppose you find that such a devotee has closed his eyes and chants the following line 101 times.

Hare Rama Hare Rama
Rama Rama Hare Hare

You may not understand the exact meaning of the ritual, or if you are familiar with the epic *Ramayana*, you will have a vague feeling that the devotee is a worshipper of Lord Rama, an incarnation of God Vishnu.

Let us forget the meaning for the time being and see if these two rituals have any outstanding peculiarities.

You need not analyse the rituals, but you will have an unmistakable feeling that both rituals are rhythmic. If you recall other rituals in other fields you will find that rhythm is the soul of most rituals. You can feel it when you watch a foreign dignitary shaking hands with the officials in a long que, you feel it when you are watching a military parade, you sense it when a gymnast shows his skill or when you are watching a swimming competition.

The words *rhythm, rhyme* or *rime* are closely related. My Oxford dictionary characterises rhythm as "regularity in the repetition in time or space, an action process feature etc...." Depending on the context the word also implies harmony, uniform flow, unison, symmetry and so forth.

Ritual Patterns

While we have identified 'rigidity', 'repetition' and 'rhythm' as the most outstanding features of a ritual or stylised behaviour it is necessary to analyse the structure of a general ritual to gain greater insight into the ritual syntax.

It is found that a ritual in general displays about 10-12 patterns. They are: *Repetition* or *iteration; palindrome* or *mirror, refrain, multiplets, embedding, relay, cycle, chorus* or *concord, pattern completion* or *structure completion,* and *overlapping.* There are also a few structures specific to a particular type of ritual.

A ritual consists of a sequence of *ritual elements* arranged temporally *i.e.,* the elements appear in series in time. The elements also appear spatially arranged or distributed in space, but the time element is more important. A game of cricket can be described fully only when you show it in space (for example, on the TV screen) but progressing in time. In many religious rituals space is an important dimension. A number of priests and the yajamana (on whose behalf a rite is conducted) may be seated only in a particular manner; idols, fruits, flowers etc. may be located according to standard rules. Fortunately, in many cases a complex ritual can be broken into simple temporal sequences.

In what follows we will use the word *subritual* to indicate an element of the main ritual, which in its own right can exist as a shorter ritual. The words *ritual* and *rite* will be used interchangeably and will apply to acts including recitations and chanting unless otherwise stated.

Repetition (Iteration)

This is an essential pattern found in any ritual. An element of ritual or a block of elements is repeated. Sometimes the whole ritual may be repeated several times.

In cricket when a batsman takes more runs than one, there is repetition of the batsman's to-and-fro movement.

A repeated chanting of a mantra is called *japa.* In a simple japa a devotee recites the name of a God continuously such as:

Rama, Rama, Rama....

Here there is a repetition of a single word. Consider a slightly lengthier mantra.

Om namah Shivaya, Om namah Shivaya.

Here the iterated block consists of three words. Sometimes the iterated block may appear at ends as in:

Om namah Shivaya Om

in which the sacred monosyllable Om appears at ends. The whole line may be repeated several times.

After the performance of a musical concert the audience applauds the performers repeatedly. The conductor in turn shows his gratitude by bowing a number of times. Here, clapping as well as bowing is an example of iteration.

Suppose you recite a mantra thrice in one sitting, then the three recitations give you the repetition or iteration of the same mantra.

Refrain

You must have come across this word when you studied literature. In verse, the word refrain means a line or a part of line or a group of lines which is repeated at the end of a stanza. In case of rituals we will use the word in a broader sense: recurrence may appear at the beginning, end or in the middle.

You should also distinguish between a refrain and repetition. In the latter iteration appears in immediate succession, there being no interruption by other words or acts. On the other hand a refrain is interspersed in a ritual, usually with regularity, but sometimes with no definite periodicity. A few illustrations may be mentioned.

(1) A factory siren hoots when it is time for the workers to start their work, when it is time to have a lunch-break, when the lunch hour ends, and finally when the factory is about to be closed for the day. Sirens are refrains, though the duration between successive two hoots may not be equal.

(2) During the roll-call, the teacher calls out the names of the students and those present say either 'yes madam' or 'present madam'. The students have two options of asserting their presence. These assertions are refrains.

(3) You walk from a pole A to pole B, making 100 to-and-fro trips. Your walking from A to B constitutes a refrain so does your walking from B to A. Similarly your taking 'about turns' through 180° at A and B are also refrains.

(4) A devotee recites a simple prayer: 'O Ganapati I hail you' five times followed by a prostration before Ganapati's idol. The whole sequence is repeated 100 times. Ganapati is an important God with the head of an elephant. The devotee's utterances followed by prostrations, 100 acts in all, are iterations, there is a refrain of the block of five utterances. His prostrations also constitute refrains.

(5) Every day you have tea thrice at 7 a.m., 5 p.m., 10 p.m. Your tea drinking is a refrain.

(6) A seller of electronic goods is explaining how a latest gadget works, to a prospective customer. During this briefing which lasts for fifteen minutes, the customer utters only a few words.

I see.. ok, ... I see... I see ... oh... I see... ok and is nodding almost continuously.

The prospective customer's nodding is iteration. His 'Oh' and 'I see' are refrains.

Palindrome

The word 'palindrome' (also called mirror, retrogade) is derived from Greek *palindromes* which means 'running back again'. In English we use it for a word, phrase etc. which reads the same backwards as forwards. It is also used to refer to a similar structure in ritual.

Napoleon the Great when captive in the prison of Elba after he was defeated, is reported to have written the following palindrome on the prison wall:

Able was I ere I saw Elba

The following examples indicate the mirror structure.

(1) You throw up a tennis ball. It reaches the highest point and returns down under the gravitational force and you catch it. Its path is a palindrome or a mirror.

(2) You walk from one pole x to another pole y, and return to the same place from where you started. You repeat the to-and-fro walk 100 times every day. We may look at your ritual in several ways:

On any one day your walking from x to y and y to x is a palindrome. There is iteration of this palindrome 100 times on any given day. On any given day you perform refrains (i) x to y and (ii) y to x 100 times. Your whole walk is a repetition which occurs every day.

(3) *Om namah Shivaya, Shivaya namah Om*

We have already come across this mantra, which is often repeated in the reverse order. It is interesting to see that a mirror like above has two parts. While *Om namah Shivaya* has the mirror image *Shivaya namah Om, Shivaya namah Om* has the mirror image *Om namah Shivaya.* However, you must note the limitations of the mirror. For instance, strictly speaking the image of Om in a mirror would look like mO. The meaning of a palindrome should be viewed with these limitations.

Another limitation which applies to this structure can be illustrated by the following ritual.

Go to college–study German–study mathematics–return home.

This can be treated as a palindrome. If we use some generalisations: the ritual can be written as:

Go to college–study–return home.

This can be treated as a palindrome though we have an extra element *study* which is not 'reflected in the mirror'. Compare this with the previous illustration where every word has an image.

Multiplets

A multiplet is a group of words or ritual acts which appears frequently in different rituals. The group appears to have a separate existence apart from its constituents.

In church music threesomes often appear as a symbol of trinity; Father, Son and Holy spirit constituting one God.

In Indian scriptures multiplets abound, and appear as triads in text, verse and rituals. Some of them are

Om namah Shivaya – 'Om hail to lord Shiva'

Om tat sat – Brahman, karmayoga, truth[1]

Bhuh bhuvah svah –'earth, sky, heaven'

Brahma, Vishnu, Mahesha–respectively, gods of creation, maintenance and destruction collectively called Trimurti. Dattatreya, a Brahmin saint, having three faces, is believed to be an incarnation of Trimurti.

According to Frits Staal triplets enjoy a special position among multiplets because three is the most common number of subdivisions of larger units. We can use the word 'multiplet' in a broader sense to connote 'singletons' such as *Amen, Amin* ('peace' in Hebrew and Arabic) and *Shantih* ('peace' in Sanskrit). You should be able to distinguish between refrains and multiplets; the former is usually a characteristic of a given ritual, while multiplets appear in different rituals. Of course some singletons like Om can belong to both categories.

End Note

[1] This is not the only interpretation. See Burde (2007), pp.76-78, 82, 87-89.

3

Ritual Patterns

A characteristic of rituals is that there are rituals within rituals and also recursive elements. Recursion, which will be considered later at some length, implies a rule by which there appears to be a built-in mechanism which tends to elongate the ritual as if by self-generation. A simple example of recursion is from mathematics. We know that 0, 1, 2... are called numbers; 1 is called the *successor* of 0, 2 the successor of 1 and so on. Thus we have: the successor of *zero* is *one*, the successor of one is two, etc. If we use 's' to denote the successor, s(0)=1, ss(0)=s(1)=2, sss(0)=3, and so on.

We can now consider other structures which characterise a general ritual.

Embedding

Consider the daily routine of a doctor attached to a hospital.

Go to hospital–visit wards–consulting–lunch–visit special patients–tea–consultation–return home.

Suppose on a certain day, say, Monday in a week, he devotes one hour to reading a medical journal after lunch. This activity can be depicted as:

Open the journal–read–close the journal.

This is a palindrome which itself is a ritual or a subritual within the main ritual. This is called *embedding*. In fact you can have a hierarchy of embedding: a ritual A in ritual B; ritual B within a ritual C and so on. What embedding demands is that the subritual and sub-subritual should be rituals in their own right.

'Pujanam' or 'puja' means a worship ritual in Hinduism. A puja may be major (long) or minor (short). In a major puja, one finds a number of minor pujas embedded. We will discuss religious ritual later.

Relay

You must be familiar with what is called a relay race in sports. When this concept is applied to rituals, relay is a pattern in which there is a chain of actors: an actor takes over the task from his predecessor and hands it over to his successor. The task is thus completed by a team.

In India those who want to protest against a law or any harsh behaviour displayed by an important official, participate in 'relay fasting'. Every person in a relay chain abstains from taking food for a certain number of hours. This type of protest gets a wide publicity because it continues for many days without endangering the participants' health.

Cycle

Cyclic phenomena abound in nature: the cycle of seasons, the cycle of national economy etc. are well known. The moon revolves around the earth which in turn revolves around the sun and so on. The behaviour of celestial bodies display a cycle within a cycle.

The characteristic of a cycle is that a ritual ends at a stage from which it started. Our daily ritual running for 24 hours is an example. Since this ritual is almost stereotyped on five or six working days, our weekly behavior has iteration of five or six cycles.

Chorus

In chorus (concord, unison), several actors perform similar activities simultaneously.

(1) *Bhajana* means singing of a devotional song. Often the song is sung by a group of devotees.

There may be a few variants of this chorus. A few singers may sing only a part of the song. Sometimes the audience joins the bhajana group and sings either a refrain or the entire song.

(2) When a play is enacted, you find that the audience responds to good acting or singing with applause. There is usually an applause when a singer, an instrumentalist, an acrobat or a speaker completes his task.

(3) In a protest march in which hundreds of people participate, you often hear the chorus of slogans: "We want justice," "Down with dictatorship," and so on.

(4) A most singular example of chorus is found when a gang of labourers is shifting a huge object. The gang-boss utters a refrain which often has no meaning. It acts as a signal to the entire gang. The whole gang responds with a similar meaningless word and simultaneously all the labourors push the object. In this case chorus is an instrument used to synchronise the individual efforts.

Pattern Completion

There appears in all of us a psychological need to finish the task which is almost complete. Accordingly we tend to complete the job so that we have a satisfaction of having achieved something. I have called this addition of the last lap of rituals *pattern completion*[1] (structure completion). Its scope is vast and involves a number of motivating factors; need for symmetry, appreciation of aesthetics, conformity with social etiquettes and norms, taboos and so on. The following examples will elucidate the concept.

(1) You are watching a TV serial which is going to end in about ten minutes. It looks as if the story is leading to an exciting climax. You have to leave for office immediately. You have always been punctual and leave home at 8.50 A.M. However. today you make an exception and wait for another 10 minutes, though you know that you will reach office late

and run the risk of being reprimanded by your boss. The pleasure of seeing the climax outweighs the opposite force *viz.* the possibility of being scolded.

(2) Your son is watching a cricket match on TV. You have decided to attend a wedding function with your family. You are likely to be late if you don't leave immediately. Your son is excited because his favourite batsman has made 99 runs. "Daddy one more run for the century, please let's wait for two minutes". You are fidgety but appreciate your son's desire to see the batsman reach the magical number of 100. Reluctantly, you decide to wait till the expected event occurs.

(3) There is a dispute between you and your wife. You feel that you need a new suit while your wife contends that you have more than enough.

You: Look, I have only three suits; brown, striped and blue.

Your wife: But you also have ten shirts.You can wear a different dress for thirty days. If you don't believe me write down the combinations.

You now realise that the same suit with different shirts make different dresses at least according to your cost-conscious wife. You start listing the different dresses: brown suit and white shirt, blue suit and black shirt, ... You can't go far since you find the task rather complicated. She gives you the entire list of thirty suit-shirt combinations. In our language of ritual she has completed the pattern.

This is not all. She reminds you that you have seven ties. 'This means you can dress differently on 210 days. She offers to write down the list of different combinations. You feel tired and wonder how your mathematician wife could arrive at the number 210 without listing the combinations. She tells you the secret. It is a matter of multiplication 3×10=30 and 30×7=210. This is a simple case of what is called permutations and combinations by mathematicians. Hence if your ritual is in wearing a suit with a tie when you are in office, completing a pattern of 'all combinations' could be one of the ways used in domestic economy.

(4) However, 'pattern completion' is not resorted to only by a mathematician's wife. Suppose you find your daughter playing with three letters, A, E, T, trying to form different words in English. She arranges two combinations; ATE, EAT, and can't go ahead. You point out the third and fourth combination, TEA, ETA.[2]

(5) Your grandmother whom you love and respect is an orthodox Hindu. You have two sons whom you have named Rama and Lakshmana bowing to her wishes. Rama is about to be married to a girl named Anushka. Your grandmother insists Anushka should be renamed Sita at the time of marriage.

In case you do not know, orthodox Hindus believe that the bride's name should be changed when she enters her husband's family, and Sita is the name of Rama's wife in the revered epic *Ramayana.*

Your grandmother is completing a pattern. In fact she started weaving the pattern when the second son was born, because Lakshmana happens to be the name of the younger brother of Rama in the epic. In all probability, when your second son gets married she will insist that his wife's name should be changed to Urmila which is the name of Lakshmana's wife in *Ramayana.*

(6) You are celebrating your silver wedding. You decide to invite your relatives and close friends of your family members; you, your wife and two grown up children. When you make a list based on the basis of this criterion, you find that of eight families in your building only one family is not listed; though the family is well acquainted with you, they are not "close friends". You feel that it would not be proper to exclude only one family from your building. Hence you decide to invite them. You have completed a pattern.

Overlapping

In a sequence of elements which consistute a ritual you often find that two successive elements overlap. For example, suppose a bank has a relay system so that its employees work in shifts. Then the rules may require that an employee should hand over the work to his reliever. This entails that the two employees doing similar work successively are present simultaneously for a short period. Usually overlapping is present to ensure continuity.

Overlapping may also effect economy in certain cases. Suppose a job is being completed sequentially by five machines. It requires some time to 'ready' the fifth machine then the operator of the fifth machine, can start working on that machine before the fourth machine completes its operations.

Recursion

We briefly mentioned recursion earlier. To understand the notion of self-embedding, consider the following example. Prostration before an idol constitutes a simple ritual. Suppose now the devotee decides to prefix and suffix this ritual by the sacred word Om, then the new ritual will appear as

Om prostration Om

This formula is obtained by modifying the first ritual viz. 'prostration'. In the next step we replace the first ritual (prostration) by the second ritual. (Om prostration Om) and we will have a 'higher' ritual viz.

Om Om prostration Om Om

If we continue the process of replacing 'prostration' by 'Om prostration Om' we will have an endless chain of rituals viz.

prostration
Om prostration Om
Om Om prostration Om Om
Om Om Om prostration Om Om Om
... and so on.

This is only one case of recursion.[3] Starting with a single ritual, prostration, and specifying the simple recursive formula: replace 'prostration' by 'Om prostration Om' we can have a longer ritual, in which the earlier ritual is embedded. This is 'self-embedding' somewhat similar to our earlier illustration of 'successor' in arithmetic.

Those of you who are familiar with computer science will realise that the process has similarity with a flow chart in which such replacements are often repeated, before you get the final answer where the chart asks you to STOP. Later you will find an illustration of recursion from a Vedic ritual.[4]

Incidentally, in the case we illustrated above, if there are no instructions to 'stop', repetition is endless and you get a ritual of infinite duration. Interestingly Patanjali was aware of theoretically infinite rituals called *sattra rituals.* While discussing recursiveness in language which leads to theoretical infinity of language, he says, "there are indeed linguistic expressions which are never used.... Even though they are not used, they have of necessity to be laid down rules, just like protracted sattras".[5]

End Notes

[1] Burde (2004) discusses this aspect in detail in chapter 8.

[2] Theoretically there are six combinations; EAT, ETA, TAE, TEA, ATE, AET, of which the third and the sixth will not be found in the dictionary.

[3] Burde (2004), chapter 7 considers several cases of recursion.

[4] Staal (1993) has considered recursion in Vedic rituals at length, pp.86-89.

[5] Quoted in Staal (1993), p.89.

4

Religious Rituals

While our behaviour is usually ritualistic, religious rituals are perhaps the most important type. It is in religion that rituals of extreme rigidity are found.

Four broad classes of religious rituals are usually recognised. *Rites of passage* which mark a transitional stage in human life are found in almost all religions. The important ceremonies take place at birth, initiation, puberty, marriage and death. *Worship rituals* may be public rituals that take place in temples, mosques, churches etc. Some worship rituals are conducted at home or privately where a few invitees are present. *Festive rituals* are usually conducted on birthdays of saints, prophets and gurus (religious teachers). The birthday of Rama or Krishna in Hinduism, Buddha in Buddhism, Muhammad in Islam and Jesus in Christianity are a few examples.

There are also *sacramental rituals* in some religions. These overlap with rites of passage, but also are conducted in relation to ordination of a religious head, public remembrance, say, of Jesus Christ, and also include confessional rituals.

Almost all patterns abound in religious rituals. Only a few examples are mentioned here.

Repetition and Refrain

(1) A *japa* of a mantra involves repetition of the mantra several times. According to *mantra shastra* (science of

mantra), the number of iterations depends on the type of mantra, the purpose for which a mantra is used etc. The prescribed quantum of repetition varies, but a japa may consist of tens, thousands and even millions of repetitions.

(2) A devout Muslim prays five times every day: on rising, when the sun reaches the zenith, its mid-decline, sunset, and before retiring. These are refrains.

(3) One of the five pillars of Islam is *Shahadah.* This is a profession of faith. "There is no God but Allah, and Muhammad is his prophet". A devout Muslim repeats it with five daily prayers and also on certain occasions. In fact Muslims pronounce the first part, *La ilaha illa 'llah* very often especially in crisis.

(4) Among Hindus every male who has undergone the initiation (*upanayana*) ceremony is required to perform two rituals called *sandhya* every day. These constitute refrains. In each refrain the following iterations are present. *(i)* Three successive oblations of water are offered to the sun. *(ii)* At the end, *Gayatri mantra* which the initiate male is supposed to memorise is recited 10, 20 or 108 times.

(5) Refrains can be observed in public worship. Worship rituals are considered important on a certain day of the week: Saturday, by Jews in synagogues, Friday, by Muslims in mosques and Sunday by Christians in churches.

(6) Rosary is a type of religions meditation. Among Catholics, Rosary of the Blessed Virgin Mary is quite important. It is a sequence of one *Our Father,* ten *Hail Marys,* and one *Glory Be to the Father* (a decade). It is repeated 5 times or 15 times. Each decade is associated with a specific meditation on some aspect of the life of Christ or Virgin Mary. It involves repetition of the entire worship formula.

(7) *Achamanam* is a ritual which appears embedded in longer rituals. In its simplest form it consists of five ritual acts: *(i)* The right palm is held in *gokarna mudra.* A mudra ('seal') is a ritual gesture and 'gokarna' is the shape of the cow's ear. *(ii)* A small quantity of water is placed on the palm.

(iii) The water is sipped off from the central portion of the palm called *brahmatirtha. (iv)* The process is repeated thrice. *(v)* A spoonful of water is taken on the brahmatirtha and discharged into a vessel.

According to tradition the achamanam should be performed *(i)* after waking up, *(ii)* after drinking water, *(iii)* when you are hungry, *(iv)* after you tell a lie, and (v) after completing lessons and so on.

Observe that both repetition and refrain are present on any given day.

Mirror

Mirror, though not as common as repetition and refrain is found in religious rituals.

(1) The following mantra is found in Yajurveda and Samaveda

Agnir jyotir jyotir agnir
Indra jyotir jyotir Indrah
Surya jyotir jyotih Suryah
(Yajurveda 3-9, Samaveda 1831)

(2) Agnichayana (*Agni* for 'fire' and *chayana* for 'piling') is a complex Vedic ritual belonging to *shrauta* type. This is also a public ritual and lasts for twelve days. In Agnichayana when each layer of the altar is built, it is preceded and followed by two ceremonies called *pravargya* and *upasad.* There are two types, both being mirrors.

Pravargya–upasad–layer construction–pravargya–upasad
or
Pravargya–upasad–layer construction upasad–pravargya

You will find that the rites before and after the layer construction are images of each other.[1]

(3) *Om dum Om* is a palindrome that appears in Durgamantra.

Multiplets

Triplets and quintets are quite prevalent. Some of them have been mentioned earlier. In sandhya which was mentioned earlier, the following triplets appear

(i) Achamana – water is sipped thrice

(ii) Arghyadana – three oblations of water

A well-known triplet *idam na mama* (not for me) appears in many rituals as a renunciation formula.

Hari Om is another duo that is used very often.

Embedding

Achamana is a self-sufficient ritual which is embedded in sandhya and also in many other worship rituals.

Relay

When there are more actors than one, relay appears when one priest "takes over" from another priest. Or a priest may ask the yajamana to complete the recitation already started.

Cycle

In a puja which is a worship ritual, many cycles appear. The devotee who is standing, circles around himself several times and then prostrates before an idol.

Devotees often walk round an idol or a temple in which idols are kept, in a clockwise direction. Each circuit is called *pradakshina.*

Mt Kailash (now in Tibet) is believed to be the abode of Lord Shiva. There is a lake called *Manas* near it. The mountain as well as the lake is visited by Hindu pilgrims. Those pilgrims who are able to make a circumambulation (*parikrama*) around the lake are believed to earn religious merit. The greater the number of circuits a devotee makes, the greater is the merit she accumulates.

In many rituals a lighted lamp or camphor is circularly moved in a vertical plane before an idol for a prescribed number of circuits. This rite, called *arati,* is also performed to honour a saint or a hero.

All the above rituals display cycles. There are also many cyclical mantras such as *Om klim hrim Om.*

Chorus

Some mantras in a ritual are recited by a number of priests simultaneously.

Multiplets such as
Om namah Shivaya
Om Shantih Shantih Shantih
(Om peace, peace, peace)
are often uttered by a group of devotees.

Pattern Completion

In certain pujas, there is a subsidiary puja in which 21 devatas (deities) are worshipped. Each deity is first offered prayer. Each of the deities is then 'invited' for the puja. In all there are 2×21=42 elements *i.e.*, each pair praying – inviting is associated with each devata, completing the pattern since all devatas should receive attention.

Affixation

In this pattern certain words, mantras or a part of mantras is prefixed, infixed or suffixed to a ritual, ostensibly to make the ritual more potent.

The most important affix is the revered word Om. There are also a number of what are called *bijamantras*, usually monosyllabic like Om, which are affixed.

As an instance of this, consider the process called activating a mantra. This is called *deepanam.* One uses the prefix *hamsa* and a suffix *soham* to the mantra:

Hamsa mantra Soham.

Soham is an extremely important mantra and Hamsa its mirror reflection.

Affixation is also used on secular occasions though to a lesser degree. For example, a renowned scholar may write a foreword for a book. A famous actor may appear as a 'guest actor' in a movie. In both cases affixation is believed to increase the value of the book or the movie as the case may be.

Overlapping

You often come across rituals which overlap. In religious rituals it is expected that there would be a continuous flow of the ritual process unless an interval for rest is prescribed. When one priest continues a ritual act or mantra already started by his predecessor, he may begin his part before his predecessor has finished. This can be attributed to the priest's anxiety to avoid any gaps in the process. Any discontinuity not prescribed in the manual, is thought to invite gods' wrath.

Of course, overlapping can also be present for reasons of economy: it may be permissible to have two processes, independent of each other, run concurrently for some duration.

Pathological Rituals

Medical literature mentions two kinds of ritualistic behaviour which cannot be called normal.

The first kind is called *Tourette's syndrome* in which a patient develops multiple tics, repetitive but involuntary urges like throat clearing, yelping, barking and so on. This disease is usually regarded as a neurological disorder.

The more important for us is the second kind which is called *obsessive compulsive disorder* (OCD) which is of interest to psychologists as well as medical practitioners especially psychiatrists. It is included here because an observer finds a striking resemblance between religious rituals and OCD, especially in respect of rigidity.

Obsessions are nagging thoughts which cannot be dislodged. For example, you may obsess that your husband's life is in danger or that if you touch your baby, she will contract a dreaded disease. You know that your fear has no rational basis, in both cases, but you cannot expel these thoughts which may create such anxiety that you may not be able to perform your routine work.

Compulsions are stereotyped acts which you may be 'forced' to do. You may have a compulsion to utter an obscene word twenty times; you may feel that you are polluted and should have bath at least five times a day. You may be forced to arrange your books in a certain pattern; you may be compelled to count from one to hundred and also from hundred to one in the reverse order. You may have compulsion to guess the ages of all the persons in your office, calculate the average age or find the difference in ages of all possible pairs that can be formed from among the employees.

Compulsions are more often than not accompanied by severe anxiety and the afflicted person may feel that a great calamity will befall her friends and relatives if compulsions are not carried out. In this respect it resembles a religious ritual. A priest usually has a dread that if ritual is not performed according to the prescribed rules he may incur gods' wrath. Usually religious manuals prescribe an expiatory ritual after the main ritual is over. The function of the secondary ritual is to tell gods that if the rules were violated inadvertently, the priest may be forgiven.

It must be realised that the main difference between the religious rituals and pathological rituals is that the former is against the wishes of the actor who cannot resist his compulsion. Sometimes he has sufficient insight to realise that these compulsions and obsessions have no rational basis, but they persist in spite of his understanding. A few examples will elucidate the complexity and rigidity of these rituals.

(1) Raman is a chemist. Every day before he goes to bed he has to clean the floor of his bedroom thrice; first with

water and detergent 'A', then water and detergent 'B', and then only with water that has been boiled previously.

(2) Embee is a student who has an urge to walk from one milestone to the next and back. Later he has to repeat the to-and-fro walk with a mantra *Om namah Shivaya.* In the third trip, he is compelled to make ten spins (circling round himself) after every twenty steps. He has to follow this procedure every day. If he cannot perform the ritual on a certain day he has to repeat the whole ritual twice at the earliest opportunity.

(3) John was born a Christian but his training in natural sciences has created certain doubts in his mind. Do the contents of the Bible agree with scientific laws? Can Genesis be a true account of Creation? His doubt gradually becomes an obsession: he starts weighing the pros and cons in respect of the veracity of the scriptures. For every statement of Genesis he lists a counter-argument from science. While preparing the list he realises that he is committing blasphemy by doubting the scripture. As a punishment he decides to write 'God exists' 1000 times every day and 'O God forgive me for my sin' 2000 times a day. As a part of punishment he also decides to list all the prophets in the Old Testament and New Testament. He is then compelled to write the year of birth and death of all the prophets and saints mentioned in the history of Christianity. This is followed by arranging the names of the saints in the chronologically reverse order. He is then compelled to classify the saints according to the nation they belonged to. He then has the urge to estimate the population of the respective nations *(i)* at the time of the birth of Jesus *(ii)* at the time of the birth of every saint in his list *(iii)* at the death of every saint in the list.

As a further atonement he decides to write down at least 200 lines from the Bible every day. He kneels down at night and must say 'religion is superior to science' 1000 times before he goes to bed.

I leave it to you to imagine the plight of the ritualist.

A characteristic of pathological rituals is that you can find almost every ritual pattern we mentioned earlier. What's more one ritual can lead to scores of other rituals which may be combined and rearranged in different patterns. The compulsive ritualist cannot stop the rituals till he is exhausted. The pain and suffering which these rituals create for the ritualist is indescribable.

Pathological rituals are structure-oriented and the actor himself does not know the meaning of rituals which may transform from one theme to another.

I have called this type *morphocentric* (Gk *morpho*, 'form').[2] On our scale of rigidity, it can be more rigid and more complex than even religious rituals. The word morphocentric does not mean centred around one pattern, it implies the importance of structure rather than meaning.

End Notes

[1] See Staal (1993), p.88 for structural details.
[2] Burde (2004), p.135

5

Mantra Patterns

Etymologically the word *mantra* means "an instrument to think". Mantras are sacred utterances that have the power to protect. Originally every word of the Vedas was considered a mantra. However, in practice there are also mantras sourced from Puranas and tantra.

According to the tenets of an orthodox school of philosophy called Mimamsa, Om is the primordial sound from which other sounds and letters were created. Om is also the source of all other mantras.

Although mantras are sacred and believed to have the power of protection, they are used for constructive as well as destructive purposes.

Types of Mantras

According to *Brahmanda Purana* there are nine methods (*vidhis*) relating to Vedic mantras. The text also mentions twenty-four 'kinds' which include praise, criticism, questions etc.

Aphorisms from Upanishads are often treated with great respect. They are called 'great sentences' (*maha vakyas*) and enjoy the status of mantras. Om and Soham are two most sacred mantras found in these texts.

Some mantras are passed on by the teacher (*guru*) to his pupil. These mantras are not to be disclosed to the public. These are called *mahamantras* (*maha* for 'great')

Many sages utter words and sentences which appear to

be ordinary on surface, but contain great power. Such *apta mantras* are picked up by those pupils who are fit to appreciate their hidden power.

Tantra texts contain many mantras which bestow siddhis or supernatural powers. They are called *siddha mantras.*

Lord Shiva is believed to have created a class of mantras for ordinary people. These are called *Shabar mantras* which are used for earthly gains and curing diseases.

Mantras have also been classified according to the number of syllables they contain. According to the text *Nitya Tantra* those mantras which contain up to ten syllables are called *mulamantras* or *bijamantras.* Those having twenty syllables are termed *kartari mantras,* while those containing more than twenty syllables are *malamantras.*

Samskaras

The word *samskara* is used to indicate a personal ceremony, but is almost synonymous with a rite of passage. Actually the word means 'polishing' or 'making perfect'. *Samskara* thus implies a process of shaping something, (including humans) according to our requirement.

Even mantras have to undergo certain samskaras, so that they are fit to be used. There are about ten samskaras which provide us with a rich mine of rhythmic patterns. In the following rituals 'mantra' means the given Vedic mantra which is subjected to various samskaras.

(1) *Jananam*: The given mantra is written on a birch leaf. A certain geometrical figure is drawn on the leaf in which are inscribed the Sanskrit letters from *a* to *ha.* The deity is then invoked.

(2) *Deepanam* involves recitation of the following derived mantra 1000 times.

Hamsa-mantra-soham

The pattern is the repetition of the above mirror or palindrome.

(3) *Bodhanam* is the japa in which the following is repeated five thousand times.
Hamsa–mantra–hamsa
The pattern is the repetition of the above mirror or palindrome.
(4) *Tadanam* consists of iteration of the following japa
phat–mantra–phat
This, again, is repetition of a palindrome. 'Phat' is a bijamantra whose significance will be considered later.
(5) *Abhishekam*
The following mantra is written on a birch leaf
Em hamsah Om–mantra–em hamsah Om
This is a mirror mantra. The leaf is then 'bathed'.
(6) *Vimalikaran* involves repetition of the following 'derived' mantra 1000 times.
Om traum vashat–mantra–vashat traum Om.
Note that the above is a palindrome centred on 'mantra'.
(7) *Jivanam* consists of repeating the following one thousand times
Svadha–vashat–mantra–vashat–svadha
The sequence is a mirror which is repeated.
(8) *Tarpanam*: In this rite the given mantra is written on a birch leaf. One thousand oblations of milk, curd and water are discharged on the leaf. The act obviously involves repetition.
(9) *Gopanam* consists of one thousand recitations of the following sequence which itself is a palindrome:
hrim–mantra–hrim
(10) *Apyayanam* consists of the japa of the following palindrome

Hsau–mantra–sauh

Note that some of the above samskaras involve recursion. For example, in Gopanam, the mantra is replaced by

Hrim–mantra–hrim

which is called self-embedding. Most of these processes also contain *prefixing* and *suffixing*.

It is believed that each of the shabar mantras is 'cursed' by different deities. To extricate and activate these mantras, about sixteen samskaras are prescribed. Even some Vedic mantras are believed to have been 'cursed' for which a number of solutions have been prescribed. In case of many mantras, it is the teacher (guru) to whom the special task of activating the mantras is entrusted.

In all these cases the mantras are affixed with bijamantras.

Gayatri Mantra

The Gayatri mantra is one of the most sacred mantras. It appears in three Vedas *viz.* Rig, Yajur, Sama. It worships Savita or the sun.

Tat Saviturvarenyam bhargo devasya dhimahi
Dhiyo yo nah prachodayat (Rigveda 3-62-10)

Three additional words called vyahritis are prefixed to the above mantra in Yajurveda. They are:

Bhu bhuvah svah

The mantra means: "We contemplate the adorable glory of the deity which inheres in the earth, sky and heaven. May he stimulate our mental powers."

The deity Savita epitomises the power of light.

Vedaghantu, a commentary, describes the meaning of vyahritis and mentions, 52, 68 and 31 devatas associated with them. Those who recite these vyahritis invoke 151 deities.

The primordial sound Om is almost always present in different versions of the japa of Gayatri.

Gayatri japa

We briefly mention below the different types of japa, which contain a number of ritual patterns. The japa can be uttered loudly or muttered (*upanshu*) or said in mind (*manasikah*).

(1) The japa is called *ekapada* when Om as prefixed. Thus Om bhuh ... prachodayat.

(2) The japa is *samputa*, when it is prefixed and suffixed with Om. Thus *Om bhuh ... prachodayat Om.*

(3) In *tripada* japa Om appears thrice.

Om bhurbhuvah svah Om tatsa ... Om dhiyo ... prachodayat

(4) The japa becomes *panchapada* when five affixes of Om are present.

Om bhuh Om bhuvah Om svah

Om tatsa ...

Om dhiyo ... prachodayat

(5) There are six Om's in *shatpada*

Om bhuh Om bhuvah Om svah

Om tatsaviturvarenyam Om bhargo ... dhimahi

Om dhiyo ... prachodayat.

In *Narada Purana* four additional vyahritis are mentioned. They are *mahah, janah, tapah* and *satyam.*

(6) *Amritasanjivani Gayatri* reads as:

Om bhurbhuvah svah Om Tryambakam yajamamahe,

Om tatsaviturvarenyam.

Sugandhim pushtivardhanam, Bhargodevasya dhimahi, Urvarukamiva bandhanat, Dhiyo yo nah prachodayat, Mrityormukshiya mamritat 'Om'.

This is an interesting Gayatri from structural viewpoint. While Om appears as a refrain, you find that the elements of the usual Gayatri are interspersed. Note that the whole mantra is also a cycle, beginning and ending with Om.

This particular method in which the components of sacred rituals and mantras are inserted in other mantras possibly arose for two reasons. First, the components were considered sacred or magical and were used to strengthen other worship mantras. Second, as time passed a few elements were detached from the original mantra and found a place in unrelated mantras, where they sometimes appear as aliens. Be that as it may, I have called this process *break - and - make.*[1]

Another structural pattern not considered earlier may be

called *generalisation* in which the deity in the mantra is replaced by other gods, goddesses and saints. For example, *Shri Ganesha Gayatri* appears as:

Om ekadantaya vidmahe 'Vakratundaya dhimahi' Tannoh dantih prachodayat

Several Gayatris in honour of Shiva, Vishnu etc. have been constructed. In some Gayatris, you even find that a 17th century saint Swami Samartha and Sai Baba, a 19th century holy man replace the original god the Sun.

If you go through the various versions of Gayatri you will find a number of ritual patterns: refrain, multiplets, affixation, cycle, repetition (of the whole Gayatri) generalisations, break-and-make, chorus (when many people recite Gayatri simultaneously). You will also notice that Om is the most frequent affix that appears in those Gayatris.

Gayatris are used for different purposes. For example, the *panchapada,* is used to cure cardiac ailments. However, we have not elaborated the uses because our stress in this book is on patterns.[2]

A few examples below will show you how mantras are manipulated structurally. It is sometimes impossible to have a semantic approach since their meaning is not clear.

(1) Can you recognise the following lines?

Yatdachopra nah yo yodhi himadhi
Sya vade bhargomanyarevaturavisatta

This is a mirror image of the Gayatri.

(2) tatsaviturvranimahe
Vayam devasya bhojanam
Shreshtham sarvadhatamam
Turam bhagasya dhimahi

This is called Savitrimantra.[3] If you inspect it you will find the elements of Gayatri embedded in it.

(3) Gayatri elements are also embedded in what are called *karanyasa* and *anganyasa* which are discussed in the next chapter.

End Notes

[1] See Burde(2004), p.203.

[2] See Burde(2004), chapter 9 for many other putative uses.

[3] This mantra is from Rigveda. For others Savitri mantras, see Sankar-acharya(1008), p.168.

6

The Sing-song Bijas

We mentioned in the last chapter that those mantras which have upto ten syllables or less are called bijamantras. However, most bijas are monosyllabic. Another significant characteristic of bijas is nasalisation. For instance the bija 'em' is actually nasalisation of the letter 'e'. It is this feature which gives a string of bijas the sing-song quality.

The French are proud of their language and consider it sonorous. French also happens to contain many nasalised words, those words which end with m, n, etc. I do not know if it is nasalisation which makes the language beautiful. If that is the reason mantras which contain many bijas with rhythmic patterns can more than match French.

Seed Mantras

The word *bija* means 'seed'. Bijamantras are also called preparatory mantras given by the guru to the newly enrolled student. There are many theories in relation to bijas. For example, each bija is believed to convey some meaning. However, these meanings are not listed in ordinary dictionaries. Many grammarians find it difficult to explain exactly what a bija means. However, there are special dictionaries such as *Bijakosha* and *Varnakosha* which explain various bijas and the power they possess. However, the power of bijas can be realised only if they are learned through a guru.

According to one theory the bija *aim* was composed from some significant words from the Vedas: *a* was borrowed from the first letter of Rigveda, *i* from Yajurveda, *a* from Samaveda and nasalisation from Atharvaveda which gives the bija aim *i.e.*, a + i + a + anusvara

The anusvara or a dot over a letter creates a bija. Four bijas *viz.* Om, eem, kleem, bloom are mentioned in the Vedas.[1]

The most important bija is Om which strictly speaking is pronounced as A-U-M. Om is also called *pranava* or *adibija* (first bija). According to some scholars it is from Om that other bijas emanated. We have already mentioned that Om is the most sacred bija which is also used as a magical catalyst. It is prefixed, infixed and suffixed to make any mantra more powerful.

The Alphabet

To fully comprehend the difference between two apparently similar bijas, say, *im* and *eem* we will use a phonetic method of spelling given below. Please note that this phonetic orthography (mode of spelling) is used only when necessary. We give below the Devanagari alphabet (which you need not memorise) along with its phonetic equivalent.

अ	आ	इ	ई	उ	ऊ	ऋ
a	aa	i	ee	u	oo	*ri*
ॠ	ऌ	ॡ	ए	ऐ	ओ	औ
ree	*li*	*lee*	e	ai	o	au
अं			अ:			
am (nasalised)			ah (visarga)			

क	ख	ग	घ	ङ
k	kh	g	gh	n

च	छ	ज	झ	ञ
ch	chh	ja	jha	n'
ट	ठ	ड	ढ	ण
t	*th*	*d*	*dh*	*n*
त	थ	द	ध	न
t	th	d	dh	n
प	फ	ब	भ	म
p	ph	b	bh	m
य	र	ल	व	श
y	r	l	v	sh
ष	स	ह	ळ	क्ष
sh	s	h	*l*	ksh

In case you do not know Devanagari here is a key to pronunciation: a (f*u*n), aa (*a*rm), ee (m*ee*t), u (p*u*t), oo (f*oo*d), *ri* (short retroflex vowel, slightly similar to the third syllable of *ability*), *ree* is longer *ri, li* is a vowel that resembles !ry in revelry; *lee* is like *li* but longer; ai (*ai*sle), o (n*o*), au (c*ow*), am (nasalisation of 'a'). A consonant can also be nasalised. For instance, bam, tam and so on; 'ah' (slightly aspirated 'a'); *t, d* etc. are similar to t, d,.. but retroflex in which the tongue is curled back. A consonant followed by 'h' indicates aspiration of the consonant. For instance, kh (wor*kh*ouse); *sh* is retroflex sh; **n** (si*n*g), *n*(a*n*d), n'(ni*n*a) or 'a girl child' in Spanish; m as in English but also used for nasalisation. You may pronounce all other consonants approximately as in English.

Unless we use this spelling, we will not be able to fully appreciate the structure earlier called "pattern completion".

Pattern Completion

Let us nasalise each letter of Devanagari alphabet:

am aam im eem um oom *ri*m

*ree*m *li*m *lee*m em aim om
aum am
kam kham gam gham **n**am
cham chham jam jham n'am
*t*am *th*am *d*am *dh*am *n*am
tam tham dam dham nam
pam pham bam bham mam
yam ram lam vam sham
*sh*am sam ham *l*am ksham

All these nasalised syllables are bijamantras. However, this is not the whole story: every consonant has different pronunciations depending upon the vowel that is added to it. Thus for "k" we have

ka kaa ki kee ku koo k*ri*
k*ree* k*li* k*lee* ke kai ko kau

Each of these can be nasalised

kam kaam kim keem kum koom
k*ri*m k*ree*m k*li*m k*lee*m
kem kaim kom kaum

Similar bijas can be formed from other consonants such as kh, g, etc. In all you will get over 500 nasals. Almost all of them are bijamantras each having a specific significance. This is a wonderful example of pattern completion where there is a correspondence between the letters (matra) of the alphabet and the bijas. Bijamantras are believed to possess distinct powers and are used in rituals when such powers are needed. For example, *hampha*t is used for protection *pha*t for destruction, *hum* for creating jealously and *khem* for black magic.

ASTRAVIDYA

The word *astra* means a 'weapon' or a 'missile'. However, it is a weapon which is activated by using appropriate rituals or mantras. The word *shastra*, on the other hand, connotes a weapon which works on ordinary principles of physics.

Sometimes, mantras themselves constitute astras. *Astravidya* is the 'science' of astras. The following are a few mantras used in astras. We need not believe in such magical mantras; the illustrations are presented mainly because they are rich in ritual patterns.

(1) *Aghorastra mantra*

Only a few lines are given below

(i) Om aghore aim aghore hreem ghora ghora shreem shravat sarvetara sarvetara rudrarupe hasaum namaste.

The stanza is full of bijas which do not have any clear meaning. But note the patterns: repetition (ghora, sarvetara); refrain (aghore)

(ii) Aghorarupe shri Brahmani avatara avatara aghorastram dehi me dehi svaha

Repetition, refrain and mirror (dehi me dehi) are quite patent.

(2) *Durgamaghorastra*

The last portion is mentioned below

Mahavira Virabhadra uvacha "hraam hreem kuru satyam shreem shreem shreem shreem shreem shreem shreem hah *th*ah hah *th*ah kha*t* kha*t* vishvakha*t* shatrukha*t* pushpakha*t* sarvajanasiddhasya kha*t* hram hraam hraum lam laam laum mana stambhaya stambhaya hraam hreem hram hraim hraum hrah Om hreem hreem shreem shreem tkreem tkreem ham jham khem khem khem ram ram ram um um um lam lam lam mam mam mam ham ham ham sarva mantra hreem hreem hreem siddhim kurukuru jhaam jheem jhoom jhaim jhaum namo namah:

Namaste namaste namaste namo bhagavate Ramadutaya sarvakrayani sadhaya sadhaya heem sarva bheeshtasarva sampattim dehi dehi hreem hreem tkreem tkreem Om Om Shreem Shreem aim aim sarvasiddhi pradaya Om hreem namah svaha"

This mantra is to be repeated 1000 times.

We do not understand most of these syllables, but we feel the rhythm and also see a number of ritual patterns;

repetitions, refrain, near-pattern completion, mirror and so on. There is one word in English which seems to verbalise its flow *viz. tintinnabulation.*

Pashupatastra

It is not possible to present the whole mantra, but a few structural characteristics may be mentioned.

From the sixth line onwards the bija 'pha*t*' appears in every line barring the last five lines. 'Pha*t*' is prefixed by a deity's name, another bija or other words.

Examples:

Om Krishna pingalaya pha*t* ...

chakraya pha*t*; padmaya pha*t*...

Hum pha*t* ...

Hoom pha*t*...

Shram pha*t*...

Sanjivaya Sanjivaya pha*t* ..., vidraya vidraya pha*t*...

Note the refrain of *pha*t. Near-pattern completion is also visible.

Nyasa

Nyasa is a method of depositing elements of mantras on various parts of the body. *Karanyasa* is the nyasa related to the hand (*kara*). For example, in tantric worship of Gayatri the mantra is broken into six parts, each of four syllables. These parts are deposited on thumbs, the index fingers, middle fingers, ring fingers and the palms. During the process of synchronisation, the word Om and the name of the body part are interspersed.

For example,

Om bhuh bhuvah svah tat savituh

Om bhuh bhuvah svah angushthabhyam namah

'Angushtha' refers to the thumb. Hence the entire karanyasa shows many patterns: refrain, affixation, break-and make etc. *Anganyasa* is similar to karanyasa but the Gayatri elements are synchronised with the heart, head and other parts of the body. Note that both these nyasas display one-one correspondence and pattern completion.

Prana Pratishtha

In many ceremonies such as puja the concerned deity is invoked and the life-force or *prana* is infused into the idol of the deity. This process is called establishment of life-force (*prana pratishtha*).

In tantric worship the process is facilitated through reciting the following mantra:

Om am hrim krim yam ram lam vam sham *sh*am sam ham hamsah soham mama hridaye bhagavati gayatri ihaivagtya sukham chiram vishthatu vaha. Om Om Om pratishtha.

During recitation the palms are placed over the heart (*hridaya*).

Note that the above is a cycle, has repetitions and refrains of Om.

Tantra

Tantra is an unorthodox method of worshipping *Shiva-Shakti* *Shiva* stands for the masculine universal consciousness *Shakti*, the female principle, literally means *power* and symbolises Mother as the goddess of power. The worship involves the use of yantras (geometrical figures) mudras (gestures) and mandalas (circles) in addition to breathing exercises, meditation, hatha yoga and mantras, most of them bijas.

Tantra literally means 'loom' or 'weaving'. It is believed that due to our defective life-style our body-mind is diseased. Tantric practice re-weaves this complex so that it regains the perfection with which it was initially designed by Mother Nature.

We have already discussed the patterns of mantras of which most of the bijas are used in tantra. We shall briefly discuss pattern completion in tantra

Tantra has an esoteric anatomy and physiology of the human body. There is a central energy channel connecting the anus and the crown. This is called *sushumna.* There are six main *chakras* located on the axis of the sushumna. A chakra is a junction where more than three energy channels or *nadis* meet. Each channel is associated with a distinct sound. The main chakras along the sushumna are (1) *muladhara* near the anus (2) *svadhishtana* at the regenerative organs, (3) *manipura* at nave, (4) *anahata* at the heart, (5) *vishuddha* at the throat, and (6) *ajna* between the eyes. At the crown is the thousand petalled *sahasrara.*

There are many pattern completions in connection with this anatomy, but we will describe only one. Each main chakra is a 'lotus' having a fixed number of petals. Each petal is associated with the characteristic bijas or phonemes, and the chakra centre too has a predominant sound. We write below the main chakras with the number of petals and the sounds associated with them in a clockwise manner.

Muladhara (4)	vam, sham, s*ha*m, sam
Svadhishthana (6)	bam, bham, mam, yam, ram, lam
Manipura (10)	*d*am, *dh*am, *n*am, tam, tham, dam, dham, nam, pam, pham
Anahata (12)	kam, kham, gam, gham, nam, cham, chham, jam, jham, n'am, *t*am, *th*am
Vishuddha (16)	am, aam, im, eem, um, oom, *r*im, *ree*m, *l*im, *lee*m, em, aim, om, aum, am, ah
Ajna(2)	ham, ksham.

Compare the bijas above with the nasalisation of the alphabet given earlier: start with vishuddha and go up to muladhara and then to ajna. In fact you are rotating the whole list about the axis in the paper and parallel to the sentences. What you get is nothing but nasalisation of the alphabet *in a proper order.* One letter is missing viz. *l* which was probably borrowed by Devanagari from the family of Dravidian languages at a later date.

It is necessary to remember that modern science has not detected either the sushumna or the chakras. Hence the tantric anatomy and physiology should be treated as a symbolic or an abstract system.

Mantra Shastra

Literally, the word *mantra shastra* means "science of mantras". It discusses the origin and nature of mantras, use of mantras and even philosophy of mantras. Unfortunately there are so many theories relating to mantras it is difficult to reconcile contradictions that appear when we try to integrate various schools.

Some theories appear to be consistent with modern science, while some are rooted in superstition and ancestor-worship. For example, structural analysis can lead to a genuine science, where the word science is used in a broad sense today.[2] On the other hand, many treatises claim that rituals and mantras when properly practiced can lead to miracles such as walking on the surface of water, flying, converting a person into a parrot and so on. Such claims have not withstood empirical tests.

One area which should interest us is the theories of sound. According to some schools sound is temporary and dies down in due course. According to some scholars, sound is eternal.

Pandit Rajamani Tigunait thinks that there are two inseparable streams of the divine; sound and light (*nada* and *bindu*)[3]. What's more, this is not only found in Indian scriptures, but also in the Bible and Talmud. Sacred sound emanates from the primordial and eternal sound called *nada*, while other sacred objects such as yantras, personified deities, mandalas etc. emerge from *bindu* (literally 'point').

The term *spanda shakti* is used to denote the inseparable duo Shiva-Shakti. Shiva is pure consciousness *apparently* static while Shakti is the dynamic power. In fact, however, the male Shiva is the potential of power which manifests as the female Shakti. Shiva is thus the ultimate source of the spanda shakti (literally, 'vibration power'). According to some thinkers the whole universe is the manifestation of vibrations: the audible sound which we here is only a small portion of the whole spectrum of vibrations.

According to the tantra tradition there is a close resemblance between the human body (microcosm) and the universe (macrocosm). Tantric sadhana which we mentioned earlier, enables the practitioner to polarize the cosmic forces with their counterparts in his body.

Tantra believes that the ultimate truth may be revealed in different equivalent forms; mantra, yantra or the corresponding deity. They even go to the extent of asserting that the triad mantra - yantra - deity has a composite existence in the sense that any one of its constituents can be converted into another. For instance, a mantra may be metamorphosed into a yantra and a yantra into the corresponding deity by a trained tantrik.

We may not believe in such metamorphosis. To us what is important is that ancient Indians highlighted the importance of vibrations and especially the fact that mantras are rooted in vibrations.

It would not be impertinent to point out that vibrations are closely associated with rhythm. Moreover most periodic motions, circular, elliptic etc. can be treated as superimpositions of different vibrations. Most of the general ritual patterns can thus be correlated with vibrations and rhythm.

Many scientists like Fritjof Capra have been fascinated by parallels between eastern philosophy which highlights rhythm and vibrations, and modern physics according to which energy and mass are interconvertible. Energy waves can be expressed in terms of vibrations.[4] The fact that even the space which appears empty contains electromagnetic waves (rhythmic vibrations) make many scientists believe that it is a vindication of ancient Indian wisdom.

End Notes

[1] See Shankaracharya (108), p.80.

[2] Those who are interested in knowing what science in a broader sense means can refer to Staal (1996), chapters 1, 2 and 6 or Burde (2004), chapter 5.

[3] See Tigunait (1996), chapter 7.

[4] See Capra (1991), chapters 14 and 15. However, some of his parallels between modern physics and eastern mystical views, such as those relating to Brahman appear to be illusory on closer analysis.

7

Language, Poetry and Prose

Language, spoken or written, is a sign system. The main function of language is communication. The Morse code and Braille are other examples of sign systems. The science which deals with such systems is called semeiotic or semeiotics. Mathematics and logic, too, have their own symbols which may be coupled with the language script we use in everyday life.

Three subsystems of a sign system are usually recognised: *syntactics* which deals with the internal structure; *semantics* which has to do with the relationship between symbols and meaning; and *pragmatics* which is concerned with the users' relationship with the system.

Language, of course, has functions other than communication, but they are less important. If you see a beautiful painting you may exclaim: "How beautiful!" though there may not be anyone nearby.

Features of Language

Language has some important features. Humans not only repeat what they have already learnt, they can *create* new expressions to suit the requirements of a particular situation. This characteristic is called *productivity*. Second, it is not iconic unlike a map of a country or a model of a machine which closely resembles what it indicates. To use the linguist's terminology, language possesses *arbitrariness* since it uses symbols that need not resemble the meaning they convey.

There are a few exceptions which you may have studied in grammar. For example, the word *ding-dong* of a bell resembles the sound of the bell. Such usage is called onomatopoeia. Because it is arbitrary, language can describe abstract thoughts. Unlike other communication gadgets, a human speaker can also receive the communication. This feature is called *interchangeability.*

Another interesting feature is *specialisation.* For example, you may witness an event, say, an accident and your knowledge arises from the coordination of different sense organs and the brain. A friend of your's comes to know about the same event through a brief account in the newspaper. In the knowledge you acquired, there was a chain of antecedents and consequences while in your friend's knowledge there was no direct functional relationship between him and the event. Such knowledge or communication which he received is called specialised.

Displacement is another feature especially important in modern days. An event which occurs in London may be recorded audio-visually and stored in a disc by you. It can be played many days after by your brother in Mumbai. This feature indicates that the antecedent and the consequence may be separated in time and distance.

Duality is the feature which connects phonemes (a phoneme is a unit of sound) and morphemes (a morpheme is the smallest meaningful element). For example, if our language had only one word 'mama' we could have only one meaningful statement 'mama'. But our language has thousands of words which can be arranged in different sequences. Some of these arrangements do not convey any meaning, but others do. With thousands of words in our repertoire we can have millions of meaningful statements using their right combination.

Finally language is *culturally transmitted.* Everything humans have created; customs, languages, machines, technology buildings and so on together constitute our *culture.* We transmit this culture from one generation to the next. This means that the next generation does not have to start from scratch. Language is the most important cultural creation–we not only teach language to the next generation, but use it to transmit culture through language. It is because of language that as time passes knowledge grows almost exponentially with every generation. Human society has been called a 'socio-cultural system' unlike other societies of animals who are said to constitute a 'bio-social system'. Animals do not have culture. Recent research suggests that higher primates may possess rudiments of culture including language, which they are able to pass on to the next generation. However, most scholars agree that even if animals do have some ability to transmit something which they themselves have created through trial and error, the level of the cultural transmission is infinitesimal compared to the human ability to bequeath culture. They simply do not have the 'hardware' and especially the brain structure which would enable them to acquire and transmit culture. You may train chimpanzees to perform relatively complex tasks and teach them elementary sign language. These acquired habits cannot be transmitted to the next generation by the trained chimpanzee.

VERSE

The word *diction* is used to connote the various facts such as syntax, words, phrases, special devices etc. used by the writer. We use the words *poetic diction* when we refer to poetry. There might be a controversy as to whether there is an essential difference between prose and poetry. Without analysing the factors which distintiguish poetry from the ordinary language, we can assert that the average reader can feel the difference between the two. It is worth quoting Thomas Gray:

"The language of the age is never the language of poetry"[1]
(Letter to West,1742)

Repetition and Refrain

English has, *inter alia,* a stress system and even in spoken English we can feel the rhythm which arises from strong and weak stresses. A characteristic of poerty is that the poet arranges the rhythmic pattern in such a way that the regular pattern recurs. It would not be wrong to say that the poet makes a poem more rhythmic than its equivalent prose. A unit of such patterns is called meter and poetry written in a meter is called *verse.* Most poets use some meter.

It is necessary to realise that a verse has multiple structures. First, since verse is a linguistic expression it is subject the syntax of the language. Of course, the poet can deviate to some extent from the standard rules: she may change the order, she may use a different spelling or even the stress system may be altered. This is done to improve rhythm, but there is a limit beyond which she cannot take liberties. Excessive deviation from grammatical rules can make a line unintelligible or ambiguous.

Second, it has also ritual-like verbal structure or syntax as we shall soon see.

Third, it has the metrical syntax resembling that of music. In fact many musical types have been constructed on the basis of metrical structures of verse.

Let us take a few example of metrical structure. The following is a line from Thomas Gray's *Elegy written in a country churchyard.*

The curfew tolls the knell of parting day

If you recite this line to have the proper rhythmic effect it will appear as:

Th*e* **cur**, fe*w* **tolls**, th*e* **knell**, *of* **par**, t*i*n g **day**

We have purposely minimised the number of symbols and used commas, which is not a conventional notation. You will find that the commas, split the line into five blocks; each block has two syllables having the same stress pattern; strong (bold) and weak (italic). Let us rewrite the sequence of stressed and unstressed syllables:

weak strong, weak strong, weak strong, weak strong, weak strong.

Observe that the pattern 'weak strong' is repeated. Each repeated block is called the *foot* of the meter. In the present case the meter used is *iambic* the most popular meter. Since the line has five blocks or patterns it is called *iambic pentameter.*

Consider another case:

Eve w*i*th h*e*r **bas** k*e* t w*as*
Deep *in* th*e* **bells** *a*nd gr*ass*

(Ralph Hodgan, *Eve*)

Try to recite the lines rhythmically and you will find that each line has two blocks:

strong weak weak, strong weak weak

Repetition of the pattern gives this structure similar to that in rituals. Note that each line also has the same structure. If you consider the entire poem, you will find there is repetition as well as refrain of the stressed and unstressed sound. This meter is called *detylic diameter* ('diameter' for 'two feet') In *trochaic* meter, the foot has the structure opposite to that in iambic and appears as '*strong weak*'. However, sometimes the last unstressed syllable is dropped, as for example, in William Blake's *The Tiger:*

Tig*er*, **tig***er*, **burn** *i*ng, **bright**

We need not discuss this topic in detail since it only introduces more and more technical terms.

The refrain in verse is also called *burden.* The first stanza of the French poem *Malbrough s'en va-t-en guerre* is:

Malbrough s'en va-t-en guerre
Mironton, ton, ton, mirontaine
Malbrough s'en va-t-en guerre
Ne sais quand reviendra, ne sais quand reviendra, ne sais quand reviendra

There is abundance of rhythm: the first and the third

lines are the same (refrain) there is refrain of a number of words. It is worth mentioning that the second line is repeated in all other stanzas and thus is a verbal refrain. You can also perceive iterations such as "ton ton".

Rhyme

Rhyme resembles refrain. For example *keep* rhymes with *peep*, and *glide* rhymes with *slide* or even with *pride.* While rhyme usually appears at the end of the lines, it can appear in the words differently positioned. In the French poem cited above, note that the syllable 'ton' occurs thrice in the second line.

In the following verse by M. Arnold, rhyme is quite patent.

Strow on her roses, roses,
And never a spray of yew
In quiet she reposes
Ah would that I did too

You must have noticed that the rhyme in the French poem mentioned above was not only at the ends but also within a line. This is called the *internal rhyme.* Consider the following:

The ice was here, the ice was there
The ice was all around.
It crackled and growled, and roared and howled.
Like noises in a swound.

This is a stanza from Coleridge's composition, and provides an excellent example of the internal rhyme.

Palindrome

Mantras are in verse and we have provided many examples of the mirror in earlier chapters. In the following lines of *Sur le pont d'Avignon,* the *mirror structure* is striking.

Sur le pont d'Avignon on y danse
L'on y danse, sur le pont d'Avignon

Palindrome, however, is not very common in English, but a metrical palindrome may be cited:

A thing of beauty is a joy forever.
Its loveliness in creases it will never.
Pass in to nothingness; it never,
(From Keat's *Endymion*)

You can easily recognise that the opening foot of the third line is 'strong weak' while the corresponding feet in the first and second are 'weak strong', giving a near-palindrome.

Sanskrit Verse

In Sanskrit, Latin and Greek the meters are *quantitative* based on the sequence of short or long syllables. A meter called *Bhujangaprayata* appears in four-line stanzas, each line having the same pattern:

short long long; short long long;
short long long; short long long.

Yor can easily identify repetition ('long' in each line) and refrains ('long long' and 'short')

Trishubha was a common stanza in the Vedas consisting of four lines (*pada*), each line having eleven syllables. The last four syllables in each line have the same cadence providing an example of refrain.[2]

Verse composed in any language has most of the patterns (metrical and verbal) which we mentioned as ritual patterns.

A singular case of refrain may be mentioned. In Dattatreya's *Avadhuta Gita* the last line of each of the twenty-two successive stanzas (Chapter IV 3-24) is

Svarupa-nirvanam anamaya ham
(I am free from disease, my form has been extinguished)

While repetition and refrain abound in poetry, other ritual patterns too are present. We have already met the palindrome. When a group recites a verse it provides an example of chorus. Mantras are usually in verse and we have already shown that they have a number of ritual patterns.[3]

We shall now show that prose or speech in general, does not share these patterns.

PROSE

We have earlier mentioned a type of Vedic ritual called shrauta. Staal has studied the structure of this ritual which is embodied in *Shrauta Sutras.* In his seminal work, *Ritual and Mantras: Rules Without Meaning,* he shows that Shrauta Sutras and Indian linguistics have considerable structural resemblance: they have similar abstract concepts such as rules and metarules (*paribhasha*); both display a hierarchical structure, and so on. Since his studies are confined to one particular class of rituals one may agree with his conclusion that shrauta rituals have a structure similar to that of language. His book also comes to other conclusions which we will discuss later.

Here we are interested in comparing ritual patterns with the syntax of language. It can be easily seen that prose and spoken language do not share these patterns, although we have shown that verse has these properties. A few illustrations will show how the use of ritual structures in prose can only have a comical effect.

(1) Before leaving for office the husband tells his wife: I I I am going to office, office, office.

(2) You ask your friend whether she had her lunch. She replies: Yes, yes, yes, at 12 noon. I had rice. I ate bread, bread and bread. Curry yes curry. I drank water, one glass, one glass more. I sipped, sipped again, again and again till the cup was empty, empty was the cup.

(3) At a marriage reception a friend presents a gift to the bridegroom with the words: "This is for you my friend, my friend. Take it my friend, my dear dear friend. This is for you, for you is this".

(4) A manager is explaining three of his sales persons how they should approach potential customers. After briefing them he asks them whether they have understood the technique. The sales persons respond in one of the following ways

(i) Abraham: We have
Sheila: understood how to
Ramu: get new customers

(ii) All three in chorus "We have fully understood your trick. Now shall we go the the field sir? Good day sir and have a nice time."

(5) There are ten students in a class. The drill master asks the monitor to form five groups, each consisting of two students. 'I shall be back in ten minutes. I should find the students in five rows ready to march. Make a list of pairs' he says. When the teacher returns he finds the students scattered all over the ground; some standing, some squatting and a few lying down. The monitor is busy writing something in his notebook. Here is what follows:

Teacher: What's is this? What did I tell you?

Monitor: You asked us to stand in five rows sir.

Teacher (cannot control his anger): And where is the row sir?

Monitor: Sir, I do not know how I should form ten groups. I am just wondering...there are exactly 45 ways in which five groups can be formed. I have started making a list of all possibilities.[3] Give me half an hour sir, and the list will be ready. You can then select the combination you feel is the best. I have already listed five alternatives sir. (shows five combinations to the teacher)

(6) A speaker at a condolence meeting: He died of cancer, God is great. He patiently suffered, God is great, for more than six months, God is great. A wonderful person. A great person. God is great. A dedicated social worker. God is great. A dedicated father. God is great. A dedicated scientist. God is great. A dedicated nationalist. God is great, great is God. May his soul rest in peace, rest in peace, rest in peace. Peace, Peace, Peace, Peace, Peace.

It is easy to see that (1) and (2) are the examples of repetition and refrain, (3) is a palindrome which is likely to embarrass the bridegroom and shock the bride; (4) contains illustrations of relay and chorus. It should not surprise us if the entire sales team is sacked. In (5) the monitor is engaged in pattern completion. I leave it to you to decide what the teacher's reaction will be; (6) shows how some well-meaning people are not able to handle a solemn occasion.

End Notes

[1] Quoted in Abraham (1993), p.163

[2] More illustrations will be found in Burde (2004), chapter 9.

[3] Given ten objects, we can make 10×9/2 pairs. This is an example of combination.

8

Music

Historians usually identify four periods in regard to the growth of Indian music; Vedic (upto 1000 BCE), Ancient (1000 BCE – 800 CE), Middle (800-1800 CE), and Modern (1800 CE onwards)

Vedic music was used mainly in chanting mantras from Samaveda. It initially used three notes to which four notes were added later.

The Ancient period saw the rise of *jatigayana* based on the text *Bharata Natyashastra* which also discussed drama and dance.

Jatigayana was supplanted by *ragasangita* based on ragas which possibly originated in *Jatigayana.* During this Middle era Indian music was also influenced by Arabic and Persian music.

While Indian classical music is still based on ragas, it has also been influenced by western music. The Modern period is characterised by experimentation and innovation, new ragas have been created and a fusion of Indian music with western music has been attempted. New instruments such as violin, piano and harmonium have been introduced into the family of Indian instruments.

Modern Indian music can be broadly divided into two branches; Carnatic (Karnataki), prevalent in the South, and Hindustani, found in the North. However, its practitioners are also found in some southern parts.

Modern Period

There are seven notes in Indian music which are called

sa re ga ma pa dha ni

These notes constitute a *saptaka* or "a group of seven". Most educated Indians are familiar with these notes and can sing the scale though they may not have studied classical music. These notes roughly correspond to C, D, E, F, G, A, B of the western major scale. There is, however, a difference in the nomenclature; saptaka is a group of seven while western musicians use the word *octave* (eight) because unlike their Indian counterparts, they include (for counting) the first note C of the next higher scale, or the *next* harmonic of C.

Technically a saptaka is divided into 22 microtones but in practice only twelve tones are important. They are:

sa (stationary)
re (soft/flat)
re (natural)
ga (soft/flat)
ga (natural)
ma (natural)
ma' (sharp)
pa (stationary)
dha (soft/flat)
dha (natural)
ni (soft/flat)
ni (natural)

A stationary (*achala*) note like sa has no variants. Some notes have two variants; natural or pure (*shuddha*), and either soft (*komala*) or sharp (*tivra*).

There are three spatakas used in Indian music; *mandra* (lowest), *madhya* (middle) and *tara* (highest). We shall use the above notations for the middle scale; a note followed by (h) or (l) will indicate the corresponding note in the next higher or lower scale. Thus sa(h) will mean 'sa' of the tarasaptaka.

RAGAS AND PATTERNS

A raga is a melodious group of notes subject to certain rules such as 'sa' cannot be omitted from a 'raga'. We need not elaborate these rules. Indian music is based on melody and the western idea of harmony is alien to it, though there is a trend in popular music to employ harmony if it contributes to euphony.

Every raga has an *aroha* (a specific sequence of ascending notes) and an *avaroha* (a specific sequence of descending notes). For example, in raga Yamana they are:

sa	re	ga	ma'	pa	dha	ni	sa (h)
sa(h)	ni	dha	pa	ma'	ga	re	sa

REPETITION AND REFRAIN

Usually in a raga there is a *mukhyanga* ('main element'), also called pakada. This is a group of notes which recur frequently. For instance in raga *Saranga* it is:

ni sa re ma re pa ma re sa

This is the refrain in this particular raga. In raga *Yamana* the refrain is

ni(l)	re	ga	re	ni(l)	re	sa
ni(h)	re	ga	re	ni(h)	re	sa

Another example of refrain pertains to what is called a *vadi* note which appears most frequently in a given raga. A *samvadi* note appears next to vadi in frequency. Thus in raga Bhoopa, ga and dha are vadi and samvadi, while in raga Durga ma and sa are refrains, being vadi and samvadi.

Kampana (vibration) is the technique of extending the same note for a longer duration, without repeating the consonant. For instance, maaa...

Obviously the kampana gives rise to iteration.

A variation of repetition appears in the style that is called *sthayi varna* in which a note is repeated as for example, in the chain.

sasa gaga nini

Here the repetitions are quite patent.

In church music *Amen* and *Alleluia* are refrains which resemble bijamantras.

It would be pertinent to mention a few differences in the nomenclature. First, a *note* in the British terminology is a sound of a definite pitch which Americans call a *tone.* Second, in Indian music a *saptaka* can be built on any base note. In western music if the scale is built on, say, D as the base it would be called 'D major' that is, D does not become C.

The above illustrations of repetition and refrain pertain mostly to classical music with notes or a group of notes as the bases of repetition or refrains. Actually when we consider longer movements we find similar structures. These can be easily identified by the lay person in popular music though she may not be able to express them in musical symbols.

Consider a simple nursery rhyme *Baa baa black sheep.* You will find that it has the structure

AB-AB

where A and B are groups of notes. Repetition and refrain are quite apparent. You may recall another rhyme "Jingle bell" and detect for yourself repetitions and refrains.

Try to sing your popular songs such as Mukesh's *Avara Hun* in Hindi or Abba's *Feranando* in English, and you will be able to find these structures without much difficulty.[1]

A pattern similar to that in "Baa baa black sheep" is found in simple bhajanas and aratis.

Palindrome

Staal cites Debussy's *Prelude No. 10* as a composition in which mirror occurs.[2] Cannonical and fugal compositions, too, contain palindromes.

Before ragas appeared, Indian music was based on *gramas.* A grama is a group of tonal sequences. A *murchana* consists of seven ascending and seven descending sequences (aroha-avaroha). For example in raga Rajani the sequences were

ni(l)	sa	re	ga	ma	pa	dha
dha	pa	ma	ga	re	sa	ni(l)

and raga *Uttaramandra* had the aroha-avaroha as

sa	re	ga	ma	pa	dha	ni
ni	dha	pa	ma	ga	re	sa

These are mirrors, and in fact there were 21 such murchanas each of them a palindrome.

In the raga system all aroha-avaroha sequences do not constitute palindromes, but some do. The sequences for ragas Durga and Shivaranjani are

sa	re	ma	pa	dha	sa(h)
sa(h)	dha	pa	ma	re	sa

and

sa	re	*ga*	pa	dha	sa(h)
sa(h)	dha	pa	*ga*	re	sa

Both are palindromes

There are palindromes in what are called *shuddha tana* which are groups of notes a singer uses. One such mirror is

sa	re	ma	pa	dha	sa(h)
sa(h)	dha	pa	ma	re	sa.

CYCLE

The palindromes discussed above (aroha-avaroha) are all cycles.

In popular music many cycles can be detected.

Mukesha's *Avara hun* cited earlier is a cycle, and so is Lata Mangeshkar's *Meri beena tuma bin roye.* If there are slight modifications in a cycle or a palindrome, *i.e.*, if the image does not exactly correspond to one or two notes we nevertheless call it a cycle or a palindrome as the case may be.

Cycles abound in percussion and western music also displays cycles which are considered later.

CHORUS

Innumerable examples of chorus can be cited in music, Indian or western, classical as well as popular.

Devotional songs are often sung by a group of devotees. This is an example of a *bhajana.* Secular music, too, is played by a group or an orchestra.

Chorus can be vocal or instrumental and many variations are found in different situations. In some cases, chorus appears only during certain parts (choral parts) of a song, and sometimes the whole audience may participate in singing certain portion, usually important refrains.

Samuhagana is the word used in India for a vocal performance by a group (*samuha*)

RELAY

Relay occurs when the song is played in sequence by a group of musicians or singers. Duets in which a male and a female sing alternately are very common in Indian songs especially those from popular movies.

There are a few variations in this pattern. While the sequence is male-female or female-male refrains may be sung by the pair giving rise to chorus.

In instrumental performance by a group, one often finds a piece played by a sequence of instruments. A special genre of Indian music may be mentioned. Two or three musicians often engage in a friendly competition. For example, a sitarist may play a small piece which is copied by a violinist which in turn is 'duplicated' by a percussionist.

OVERLAPPING

We have already mentioned that in a religious ceremony it is usually ensured that there is no discontinuity or *horror vacui.*[3] Avoiding gaps may be prompted by the fear that any discontinuity will attract gods' wrath. Many mantras are set to tune (for instance, those from Samaveda). When one priest follows another, he may begin before his predecessor has completed his part. Generally it is the anxiety of not 'taking over' from the predecessor which makes a priest start chanting before the appropriate time.

However, in some popular music overlapping is also used as a technique in which a small interval of time sees two or three players participating or the relay is deliberately converted into overlapping for a short time.

Incidentally overlapping is found even in ritual acts not amounting to chanting or reciting.

Staal mentions a simple example of overlapping motives from Mozart's *Sonata for Violin and Piano* K 402. Overlapping is also present in counterpoint and polyphonic music. [4]

MULTIPLETS

Triplets like 'Buh bhuvah svah' are found in abundance in Indian mantras. When tuned to music (as in case of Samans) they appear as musical triplets. Other examples are *Om namah Shivaya,* and *Hare Rama, Hare Rama, Rama Rama, Hare Hare* in devotionals music.

MINUET, RONDO AND SONATA

In classical western music one finds an interesting ternary (consisting of three elements) structure called Minuet which can be depicted as A B A. You can easily make out that it is a palindrome. The central section is usually called the *trio.* Minuet was originally a European court dance of 17th century leisurely in triple time which ultimately found a place in many forms of musical pieces. A *rondo* appears as an extension of the ternary form, say, as ABACADA which is a cycle in which three palindromes are embedded.

Sonata is an instrumental piece in three or four movements. The first movement is called Sonata Form which consists of three elements; exposition, development and recapitulation and is almost a mirror. The second element is a minuet (optional) or a scherzo (which is a triple time like minuet but faster). The last element of sonata is *finale.*

In the structure of rondo mentioned above, if D is replaced by B we get a form ABACABA which is called *sonata-rondo.* Observe that it is a mirror. If you inspect it carefully you will find no less than three palindromes (mirrors) embedded in it.

Harmony – Harmony uses *chords* or simultaneous sounding of two or more notes. However, chords is not a mere collection of multiple notes, their progression constitutes musical syntax.

Some critics maintain that harmony is a mere clothing of melody. However, many others point out that it has its own enriching contribution. For instance if Beethoven's music is stripped of harmony it would cease to be what it is: a musical product of a genius.

We have already mentioned that Indian conventional music does not use harmony. However, modern popular music has adopted this technique and it is a matter of time before harmony is naturalised in Indian music.

SYMPHONY

Symphony (lit 'sounds together') in a broad sense means music in which different instruments create a euphoneous piece.

In a restricted sense, it is an 'orchestral sonata' consisting of four movements: the first is a substantial portion, the second has the same mirror structure as the third. The fourth movement is a modification of Sonata Form. It is a bit complex and follows what is called the 'transformational rule'.

We need not discuss this form.[5]

EMBEDDING

We have already mentioned embedding which occurs in music along with other structures. We have also pointed out that a minuet is a triple and a palindrome. Each element of this triple has the same structure (A B A) as the minuet itself. This is an excellent example of embedding of palindromes into a palindrome.

RAGAS AND MUSICOLOGY

There is no doubt that Indians possess a penchant for classification and manipulation of figures. This is reflected in systematic development of musicology or science of music. In this context pattern completion needs special attention since it is based *inter alia* on permutations and combinations.

While there are a number of illustrations in this field we shall particularly mention the contribution of the seventeenth century Karnataki musician Vyankatamukhi.

We have seen that a note can have more variants than one. For example, sa has one variant while re has two variants. Vyankatamukhi considered the number of variants of different notes in a saptaka. How many sequences can be obtained from a saptaka? This is a simple problem in permutations and combinations.[6] The answer is 32. Each of these sequences was called a *thata*. Vyankatamukhi went further and created two euphonic blocks each of four notes. For example, sa *re* re ma and pa *dha* dha sa(h) are two illustrations from the first and second block. There are six combinations in both blocks. If you join a combination each from block 1 and block 2 you get a sequence of eight notes. In the above example, the sequence is

sa *re* re ma pa *dha* dha sa(h)

How many such sequences are possible? The answer is 6×6=36. Now, in Block 1 ma is *shuddha.* If we replace it by ma *tivra* we will have additional 36 varieties giving us in all 36+36 or 72 thatas.

Note that such constructions are purely theoretical and a thata can be considered purely a parameter which has no physical correlate. However, there are some ragas called *ashraya ragas* or *janaka ragas* which have a correspondence with thatas. For instances raga Todi has aroha-avaroha as

sa	*rega*	ma'pa*dha*	ni	sa(h)
sa(h)	ni*dha*pa	ma'*ga*	*re*	sa

which is a replica of the corresponding thata.

In Hindustani music, however, there are only ten thatas from which different ragas can be composed.

End Notes

[1] In order to avoid a plethora of symbols only a few illustrations are presented here. For deeper analysis and more illustrations, see Staal (1993) or Burde (2004).

[2] See Staal (1993), p.191.

[3] Those who can follow western notations may refer to Staal (1993), p.171 for more illustrations of overlapping.

[4] Ibid., p.171.

[5] For details see Staal (1993), p.174.

[6] The problem involves the product of the variants of the notes: 1×2×2× 2×2×2 = 32.

9

Percussion and Dance

When we hear a piece of music, most of us react rhythmically; we may drum, tap or make some periodical thud. What we are doing spontaneously is what a percussionist does professionally. Rhythm means 'flow of music' but it is the time element which we stress when we speak of rhythm. Music has three most important characteristics; melody which has to do with the pitch of notes, rhythm which is related to patterns in time, and harmony in which chords are used. The first two features, however, are universal and are found in the music of any society. Some types of music such as Indian classical music lack harmony, but have melody and rhythm.

If you delete melody, what remains in this duo is rhythm. Rhythm also appears outside music in many universal phenomena that we call 'periodical'. Percussion instruments are the means of highlighting rhythm. A percussion instrument like tabla has little melody but can produce a plethora of rhythmic combinations. In particular rhythm brings together music, dance, percussion and verse. They seem to form a family whose members live happily in unison. What's more, they also share many ritual patterns. Only, in some rituals rhythm may not be perceived easily but all rituals have rhythm which is reflected in ritual patterns.

Percussion in Hindustani Music

Indian classical music has a well-developed art and science

of percussion. The word *tala* is used to indicate a rhythmic pattern. The interval between two beats is called a *matra.* This is roughly equivalent to a tone.[1] 'Laya' is analogous to tempo or speed. There are three speeds in Hindustani music; slow (*vilambita*), medium (*madhya*) and fast (*druta*). We may tanslate tala as 'meter'. A tala is divided into *khandas* or sections.

A tala of percussion is called *barabara* (equal) if it agrees with the tempo of raga music. If there are twice as many beats in the same interval, it is called *duguna* and the one having four times faster than *barabara* is *chauguna.*

Tabla

We shall briefly discuss the percussion patterns with reference to *tabla* the most post popular instrument of percussion in Hindustani music.

A tabla consists of two drums called *dagga* and *tabla* to be struck with the left and right hand.

A distinct feature of the tabla pair is that nine basic sounds (for example, *ta, na,* ...)can be obtained from the tabla drum and four sounds can be struck with the dagga (*gi, dhi,* ...). These sounds are called *varna* or *bola* Over twenty complex sounds (*tak, tirkita,* ...) can be created with the combination of these bolas.

A few talas can be mentioned. *Eka tala* (*eka* for 'one') has six *khandas* and two beats in each khanda, in all 12 beats, and can be depicted as 2,2,2,2,2,2,

Similarly a few other talas are as follows:

Kerava 2,2

Rupaka 3,2,2

Zapatala 2,3,2,3

Note the repetition of 2 in the first three, and refrain in the last.

If you think this is a trivial example, we write below a few examples of pieces called *theka, peshakara* and so on which consist of complex sounds we mentioned earlier.

1. *Peshakara* (Ekatala)

Dindha dhati dhadha dhindha dhati dhati dhadha dhindha.

Tinta tati tata tinta dhati dhati dhadha dhindha

The second line is a near-repetition of the first. You will also see repetitions of constituents like dhindha. The first line is also a cycle.

2. *Peshakara* (tintala)

Dhati dhadha kridha dhati dhadha kridhan dhadha dhindha.

tati tata krita tati dhadha kridhan dhadha khindha

Here again there is a near-repetition of the first line in the second. Note also refrains of dhati, dhadha, etc.

3. *Kayada Rela*

Dhirdhir dhidanaga dhirdhir
dhidanaga tina kidanaga
Dhirdhir dhidanaga dhirdhir
dhidanaga tina kidanaga
Tirtir dhidanaga tina kidanaga
tirtir kidanaga
Tirtir dhidanaga tina kidanaga tirtir kidanaga
Tirtir kidanaga tina kidnanaga dhirdhir dhidanaga
Dhirdhir dhidanaga tina kidanaga

There is repetition of the first line and many refrains. There are also internal repetitions and rhymes.[2]

DANCE

Humans and animals respond to lively music rhythmically, their body movements appear cyclical and can be shown to display most of the general ritual patterns. This response is instinctual and in case of humans it flowers into dance.

Dance, music and beats appear almost inseparable. In fact the idioms for dance and music are almost identical. Musical terminology can be used in dance and *vice versa.*

Dance may be solo or performed by a group. There are

folk dances, ballroom dances, classical dances and ballets. Dances may have different purposess, religious, ritualistic and so on. While the ritual instinct is more prominent in most dances, some dances are specially designed to convey a story or myth as in case of a ballet. In most classical Indian dances, apart from the beat of steps, interpretation of body movements and especially facial expressions are of importance.

Since the pattern of musical beats is translated into the foot-steps in most dances, the dancer's steps are the most important characteristic pattern in a dance. In many dances such as tap dances and Indian classical dances, the 'step-beats' are audible and have to be in consonance with percussion beats.

Repetition and refrain are, of course, the most important ritual patterns as in case of music. The repeated block is sometimes called a cycle (which has a slightly different connotation in our terminology).

We may legitimately call the pattern of step-beats the *acoustic syntax* or *percussion syntax*, which is, of course, connected with the flow of music. However, the body movements, too, give rise to a syntax which displays most of the ritual patterns.

Western Dance

Many of you may be familiar with ballroom dances. These are social dances of which about nine types are recognised for world championships; waltz, tango, foxtrot, quickstep, samba, rumba, cha-cha-cha, paso doble and Viennese waltz.

Foxtrot is a popular dance which is quite lively. It is of American origin. Performed by duos (couples), it is in duple time *i.e.*, two beats in a bar: 2/8, 2/4, 2/2, (simple duple) or 6/8, 6/4 (compound duple). Ravel has written a dance in the opera *L'enfant et les Sortilèges* (1925). *Quickstep* is a fast version of Foxtrot.

Waltz is one of the most popular dances of Austrian origin. It is in triple time *i.e.*, three beats in a bar, 3/8, 3/4, 3/2 (simple) or 9/8, 9/4 (compound triple). It is popularly known as the three-step dance.

Mazurka is a Polish dance in triple time of changing pace. It is usually stressed (accented) on the third beat. Chopin has written more than fifty mazurkas.

Rumba is a lively dance of Afro-Cuban origin. Its usual rhythm is 4/4. *Samba* is a Brazilian dance quite lively, which is syncopated in its duple rhythm. In *syncopation* there is a displacement of the usual accent.

It is extremely difficult to assess ballroom dances from the viewpoint of prestige. Being social dances, they may be treated as the common man's mode of entertainment. Nevertheless, some of the dances have been written by world-renowned composers. The fact that there were court dances also shows that the social dances had a status dependent on where you danced rather than what you danced.

Ballet is usually regarded as the most refined form of dancing. Like opera it tells you a story and is performed with orchestra. There is neither declamation nor singing. The audience understands the story through dance movements with appropriate music. It is of French origin. Some of the greatest choreographers and composers have created well-known ballets: *Les petits riens* (Gluck and Morzart), *Swan Lake* (Petipa and Tchaikovsky.) So respected is the ballet today that it has a place in opera and musical shows in which they appear as dance sections. In Britten's opera *Death in Venice* (1973), one of the the principal characters is not a singer but a dancer.[3]

The close affinity between music and dance cannot be exaggerated. The very word 'orchestra' comes form a Greek word which means a dancing place. Many musical structures have origins in dances. The minuet which we mentioned in the chapter on music was actually a European court dance in a languid triple time.

Indian Dance

Bharata's *Natya Shastra* is perhaps the world's oldest text on dramaturgy, and most classical Indian dances claim to have originated in this *magnum opus.* Indian dance is not a mere sequence of rhythmic movements, it has many dimensions: rhythm, aesthetics, story telling, expression of emotions, philosophy and spiritualism. This shows that qua ritual it is not meaningless unlike the shrauta ritual. It is a designed ritual in which the states of mind (*bhavas*) are of great importance. A bhava may be expressed through words, gestures and facial expressions. It is the combination of bhavas which produce a *rasa* (literally 'juice') or emotional states such as Shringara (Erotic), Raudra (Furious) and so on.

Rhythmic or ritual structures appear in Indian dance at various levels; music, dancer's steps, and body movements. The main two features of Indian dance are pure dance (*nritta*) and enactment (*abhinaya*). Some scholars consider three aspects of dance viz. *nritta* or pure dance which has only rhythm (*tala*), *nritya i.e.,* dance with emotional expressions, and *natya,* which contains abhinaya *i.e.,* interpretation of gestures. In a short discussion below, we will borrow from *Bharata Natyam,* a renowned style, and treat this type as a representative of classical Indian dance.

Unfortunately it is difficult to isolate structure from semantics in Indian dance since it is an integral whole whose elements; steps, bodily movements, music and words cannot be discussed either separately from each other or from the theme. Nevertheless we shall try to highlight the structural aspect of the dance.

The most important 'unit' of movement is *chari,* or the movement of one foot. There are thirty-two types of chari of which sixteen are terrestrial (when the foot is in contact with the earth) and sixteen are aerial (when the foot is in the air). *Karanas* are movements of two feet of which there are 108 varieties. They are also classified as either terrestrial or aerial.

The basic dance step in Bharata Natyam is *adavu* which is a combination of pose (*sthanaka*), chari and a hand movement (*nritta hasta*). A rhythmic sequence of adavus gives rise to a pattern called jati. A khanda is a group of *karanas* and the pattern of three or four khandas is called a *mandala.*

Before a dancer begins a real piece of dance, she thoroughly learns various adavus. For example, *tattu adavu* is a sequence of seven or eight steps in half-sitting position (*aramandi*). The dancer alternately strikes her right foot and left foot on the floor according to the beat. Each adavu has a distinct *bola.* In *tattu adavu* it is *tai ya tai, tai ya tai.* Even in such a basic step the ritual patterns are patent: an iteration of 'left-right' and refrains of left and right. In *nattu adavu* which has twelve steps you also find pattern completion inasmuch as there are various stretches by one foot, the other being stationary on the heel. The roles of the feet are then reversed. In *tatti mettu adavu* there are refrains of strikes and jumping steps. There is also a repetition of four beats: *tat tai ta ha.* (Remember that repetition of a sequence is also called a cycle in one sense.)

In certain pieces one also finds multiplets especially triplets called *arudi* which mark a transition, say, from nritta to nritya. Pirouette-like cycles can be seen in the steps called *sutral adavus.*

In Bharata Natyam and other Indian classical dances there is complex but beautiful integration of several rhythms: music (insrtumental or vocal), percussion (mridangam) and the steps which follow the *nattuvanar's* cymbals.

Rhythm and Dance

As we mentioned earlier it is extremely difficult to separate *abhinaya* from pure dance. Even from the structural point of view *abhinaya* has a place in the whole complex syntax:

the dancer maintains rhythmic cycles though this may not be obvious if you are a novice and have not learnt the art and science of dance appreciation.

In Carnatic music the rhythmic patterns are called *jatis.* The basic jatis or groups of beats (matras) are as follows:

Jati with number of beats	Bola						
Chatusra (4)	ta	ka	dhi	mi			
Tisra (3)	ta	ki	ta				
Misra (7)	ta	ka	dhi	mi	ta	ki	ta
Khanda (5)	ta	ka	ta	ki	ta		
Sankareena (9)	ta	ka	dhimi	ta	ka	ta	
				ki	ta		

A *tala* is a rhythmic pattern. There are seven basic talas which can be shown as follows:

Tala	Syntax
Dhruva	1011
Matya	101
Rupaka	01
Jhampa	1U0
Triputa	100
Ata	1100
Eka	1

1 is called *laghu* and indicates a strike of the palm followed by the remaining number of beats of the jati you are using. These beats are counted on fingers. 0 stands for *dhrutam* which consists of one strike of the palm and one wave of the hand. U is called *anudhrutam* and denotes one strike of the palm. To simplify matters suppose you use only one jati in a particular tala. Since there are five jatis and seven talas you get 35 (7×5) combinations of tala-jati. Here is an example of pattern completion using only one-one combination between the basic talas and jatis.

Suppose you are using tisra jati in jhampa tala which has the structure 1 U 0 . Since the tisra has the bola *ta ki ta,* a complete cycle will have the pattern X ** XX˘

where X stands for the strike of the palm; * for the counting on the fingers and ˘ for the wave of the hand. The cycle pattern is called *aavartanam.* The tisra in jhampa tala will yield six beats in all

1(3)+U(1)+0(2)=6

You must, however, remember that only three (X) beats are struck or audible beats, the remaining are silent. If there is another combination giving six beats, it will not have the same pattern. For example, consider chatusra in rupaka tala. The latter has the structure 01. Since the chatusra has four beats, the pattern of the aavartanam is X ˘X ***

The number of beats in the aavartanam is 0(2)+1(4)=6. Nevertheless, it has a pattern different from that of the tisra in jhumpa.

It is these basic talas which determine the manner in which music is played and the way the dancer structures her steps.

Gati roughly means speed and in dance it shows variation in the duration of the beats. Gati is classified in the same ways as jatis and thus can have 3,4,7,5,9 unitary durations. Gati introduces a dimension which makes the structure immensely complex. Some talas have more than two hundred beats while some tala groups use fractions of beats. Fortunately, such complex structures are either used in music alone or have only a theoretical importance.

The talas often used in dance are *adi tala* and *misra chappu.* The former resembles chatusra jati triputa but has a cycle of 16 or 32 beats.

In chappu tala the only variable is the time measure. A variant of tisra jati triputa is called *misra chappu* which has the beat structure 3+2+2. Since other parameters (angas) are not important in chappu, jatis determine its pattern. Thus the tisra has three beats while the khanda has five.

Tala Prana

A tala usually has many variables (angas) which introduces structural nuances.

Kaalo is the tempo of which, like Hindustani music there are three; vilambit, madhyam and drut having the ratio of beats 1:2:4.

Marga indicates a particular tradition or style in which a rhythm is played and may be called a particular school (*gharana* in Hindustani).

Kriya indicates the way a tala is played *i.e.*, how you express a tala using different gestures such as counting, clapping, etc.

Angas are the limbs of tala of which the most important laghu, anudhrutam and dhrutam have already been mentioned.

Jatis: We have mentioned the five jatis having 3,4,7,5,9 beats.

Kalaa shows how a cycle (aavartanam) is played. A beat for instance, can be played once, twice, thrice or four times which incidentally, gives rise to repetition.

Laya shows the variation of intra-aavartanam tempo.

Yatihi resembles onomatopoeia: the structures try to mimic various sounds found in Nature.

Prastara is a parameter similar to pattern completion: it uses permutations and combinations provided certain basic rules are not violated. For example, a rhythmic cycle should always terminate with *teehaiyee* (a beat pattern repeated thrice) which is at once a multiplet and repetition.

Dance Performance

Apart from the dancer(s) there are other persons who accompany the main performer; the percussionist who plays *mridangam* (drum), *nattuvanar* who directs the dance and also uses cymbals, flautist or a violinist and the singer.

It is necessary to remember that there are different rhythms of the song, mridangam and cymbals. The dancer follows the *nattuvanar* to 'interpret' the whole complex of different patterns. To the aesthete a good dancer is one who combines different elements with her abhinaya in such a way that what unfolds before an aesthete is a beautiful *One* in which diversity seems to disappear.

Dance is all rhythm, in fact, it is a rhythm of rhythms. It displays all ritual structures mentioned earlier in verse, music, percussion (sometimes more sequences than one depending on the number of instruments used) and the movements of the body. The body and limbs execute patterns similar to those in exercises and gymnastics. The head moving to and fro or sideways shows repetition and palindromes. Pirouettes and their equivalents exemplify cycles. In group dances there are choruses and relays. There are also instances of overlapping as modifications of a relay. Different postures and movements using all possible combinations demonstrate pattern completion. Bowing or saluting in the *namaste* posture are multiplets. In a given type of dance many stylised movements and postures appear as *refrains.*

You may analyse a dance for ritual patterns in different dimensions; verse, music, percussion beats and the beats of the steps, bodily movements and so on. A holistic view would reveal to you a rhythm which coordinates these different dimensions and their individual rhythms.

There is another aspect found in a classical dance like Bharata Natyam. The entire recital is presented in a sequence of pieces starting with *pushpanjali* or 'offering of flowers'. Each section lays emphasis on different dimensions of the dance. For example, in *alarippu* following the pushpanjali there is neither a song nor a melody but only dance syllables. In *jatisvaram* there is a synthesis of jatis and notes of the raga. In *varnam* nritta and abhinaya (which cannot be divorced from dance) occur alternately.

The other classical Indian dances (or dance dramas) are Kuchipudi (Andhra Pradesh), Mohini Attam (Kerala), Odissi (Orissa), Manipuri (North-Eastern India), Kathak (North India), Kathakali (Kerala).

We mentioned in the beginning that Indian dance has a spiritual dimension. Most of these dances borrow from religion and mythology. God Shiva whose abode is believed to be Mt Kailash in Himalayas, is called Nataraja, the Lord of Dance. His Tandava style of dancing has become an epitome of dancing. It is believed that through Tandava, Shiva creates, sustains and destroys the world.[4]

End Notes

[1] A tone is strictly speaking a major second or twice a semitone. A major second is the interval between such notes as C and D, both included.

[2] Many more pieces will be found in Gajendragadkar (1992), chapter 7.

[3] You can find more information in Headington (1983), pp.18-19.

[4] For a detailed account of myths and legends connected with dance, see Sahai (2003), chapter 3.

10

Sports, Games and Recreation

There are a number of rituals which can be subsumed under health and recreation. Apart from dance and music, they include physical exercise, swimming, gymnastics, sports in general, and games. Of course, these subgroups are not water-tight compartments. Similarly health and recreation are not mutually exclusive. All these activities display general ritual patterns of which repetition and refrain seem to be essential structures.

We can only briefly discuss this topic: most of these activities are so full of rhythmic patterns that no elaborate analysis is required.

Physical Exercise

The easiest exercises are running and walking, especially brisk walking. Your hands as well as legs move rhythmically displaying iteration as well as refrains. Their to-and-fro swinging trajectories are palindromes and may also be considered as cycles. When you perform walking or running in a group, there is chorus.

Consider the following exercises for strengthening various parts of the body.

(1) Lie flat on the floor keeping your arms at the sides. Bend your head forward through 90° till the neck is vertical, then bring back the head to the original position. The shoulders should not move during the exercise.

(2) Stand erect, thrust the chin forward. Pull it backward as far as possible. Repeat.
(3) Stand erect. Lower the head towards the chest. Rotate it to the left rolling it back to the right and to the original position. Repeat the rotation in the clockwise way. Repeat the whole sequence.
(4) Raise the arms above the head in the standing position, palms facing you. Circle the hands first bringing them down and then up to the original position in a wind-mill fashion. For a wider circumference you may use each arm alternately.
(5) Stand erect. Bend forward so that your hands touch the ground. You should simultaneously raise your right leg behind. Go back to the original position. Repeat, raising the left leg behind.
(6) Stretch your arms overhead. Bend to the left as far as possible and then to the right and back to the original position. Repeat.
(7) Lie down, raising your legs pointing upwards. Move your feet in a horizontal circle. Repeat.
(8) Stand with your arms at sides at the shoulder level. Describe vertical circles with both your hands.

Repetition occurs in all exercises; refrain in most of them. Palindrome is present in walking, running, and in (1), (3), (4), (5), (6). Cycles occur in almost all exercises, (7) and (8) giving full circles. When done in groups, chorus can be said to be present.

If you recall scores of exercises you did in your school especially under the drill instructor, you will find that all exercises contained iterations, most had refrains and mirrors, many contained cycles. All the exercises when performed in groups had chorus. Many had 'embedding'–the shorter exercises embedded in the longer. If you inspect these exercises you will even find pattern completion. For instance, such variations as hands held vertically upwards, hands held sideways, hands held horizontal in front provides a pattern compleition. The characteristics of such variants is that limbs are positioned or circled in many possible ways, but the type of the exercise is similar.

Gymnastics

Many physical exercises can be performed with the help of implements: dumb-bells, weights (in weight-lifting), bars(single or double) and many other implements. In gymnasium you will be able to find all the patterns in the movements of the gymnasts.

Gymnastics has recently acquired a new esthetic dimension, one sees artful movements in addition to agility. These include walking on toes, somersaults, various twists and many other graceful movements. All these display simple or complicated structures which contain most of the ritual patterns.

Sports and Games

If you have watched the game of cricket which is immensely popular in many British Commonwealth countries, you must have observed many patterns: repetition of 'overs', innings and matches, refrains of bowling and batting which are more regular and refrains of less frequency such as catching, stumping, umpire's signals and so on. When a batsman takes more runs than one, there is iteration, mirror and cycle. You also find the chorus of 'How is that'. There is relay when one batsman takes over from another who is out. Similarly when an 'over' is complete *i.e.*, when the bowler has bowled six balls he hands over that department to another bowler.

Consider another indoor game, table-tennis also called ping-pong. The ball moves to-and-fro, it also strikes the table periodically. There is alternate hitting by two players. There are refrains of 'service', 'netting', alternate aggressive and defensive playing by the two adversaries. You will find most patterns; repetition, refrains, palindrome (to-and-fro movement of the ball), relay (one player takes over the 'service' from another). When the game is played in 'doubles', two pairs on each side, you have similar patterns. You even find pattern-completion in how the game is played: 'singles', 'doubles', 'mixed doubles'. There is further room for pattern completion: man vs. woman, men vs. women, but in sports division by sex is considered important *i.e.*, males and females are considered different classes.

In swimming competitions, too, you find repetition, refrains, palindromes (to-and-fro), chorus (simultaneous performance), and so on. Watch the movements of the hands, legs and the head, there is repetition, refrain, cycle and palindrome in various styles of swimming: free style, breast stroke, back stroke, and butterfly, etc. In medley you find the pattern completion in addition to relay. (one style giving way to another).

Relay is a structure found in what is called the 'relay' race which is a track event.

In automobile races, circuits or laps provide an example of a cycle. In a bicycle race there are cycles of the feet and wheels, and of course, repetition. Application of brakes demonstrates refrains.

In skipping, the rope performs cycles; your feet make repetitions of a palindrome (up and down). With a little dexterity the roap can be looped through which you execute your jump. The loop occurring once in a while gives rise to a refrain.

Even such a simple toy as a yo-yo can display repetition, refrain and palindrome.

Watch the most popular track event in sports, running. There emerges a complex rhythm involving the movements of four limbs. You can easily identify patterns executed by each limb or a conjunction of limbs; repetitions and palindromes being predominant. Variants like hurdle race introduce refrains where you have to overcome the hurdle.

Symmetry

One of the reasons why ritual patterns abound in human activities is that we have a symmetrical anatomy, the left part of the body is a mirror image of the right and *vice versa*. If we had only one hand and one leg, we would not be able to perform many rhythmic movements. Symmetry also introduces a conjoined pattern of similar pairs, the left hand and the right hand or the left leg and the right leg. You will notice that many ritual patterns in time have correlates in spatial patterns.

11

Rituals and Space

Earlier we mentioned that a ritual, strictly speaking, can be described fully when its spatial dimension is also considered. Interestingly, we find that many ritual patterns described earlier have correlates in space. We can only briefly discuss this aspect with special reference to tantra in which a plethora of yantras display in space patterns similar to ritual patterns in time.

Yantric Patterns

We shall discuss yantric patterns with reference to some of the most important yantras. According to some tantric texts the primordial sound (*nada*) was 'ekoham'. This sound gave rise to the point (*bindu*). The bindu is found at the centre of many yantras.

It is believed that the bindu expanded and became the 'expanded point' (*vriddhabindu*), circular in shape. The bindu when perceived as the seed of a circle (*chakra*) is called the potential of the circle (*chakra sambhava*).

The first sound was followed by another sound *bahushyam* which created pashyanti, madhyama and vaikhari elements within the circle. These elements gave rise to chakras *trailokya-mohana, sarvanandamaya* and so forth. Tripurasundari is the goddess of these chakras. Sri Yantra, perhaps the most revered yantra in tantra, is associated with this goddess, also regarded as Mother.

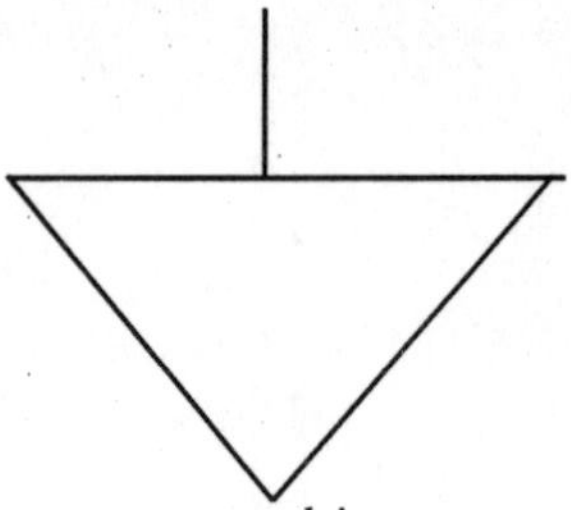

Fig. 11.1 Shringataka Trikona

The triangle called *Shringataka Trikona* is also believed to have originated from the bindu (Fig. 11.1). The bindu with linear expansion became a line. The vibrations of this line led to formation of two more points *vama,* identified with Vishnu and *jyeshtha,* identified with Agni (fire god). These points are also associated with *sattva guna* (righteousness) and *tamas guna* (dullness). When the powers (*shakti*) of these points dissolved, a new shakti called *raudri bindu* associated with *rajas guna* (activity) emerged. The triangle formed by these three points symbolises the union of three characteristics; will, knowledge and action and also light, life and love.

The point, triangle, square and petals frequently find a place in the geometry of yantras. We will not discuss the symbolic meaning of these elements, but concentrate on the structural aspect of a few yantras.

Figures 11.2, 11.3 and 11.4 show some of the most renowned yantras used in tantra. They are Sri Bagalamukhi (a goddess) yantra, Sri yantra already mentioned and Sri Maha-mrityunjaya (*maha* for 'great', *mrityunjaya* for 'the conqueror of death').

Repetition

The spatial counterpart of repetition is occurrence of the same figure or symbol successively. In the figures you can easily identify repetition of petals in all yantras, so is the iteration of circles in Figs. 11.2 and 11.3. Repetition of the border design is found in all these yantras.

Fig. 11.2 Sri Bagalamukhi Yantra

Fig. 11.3 Sri Yantra

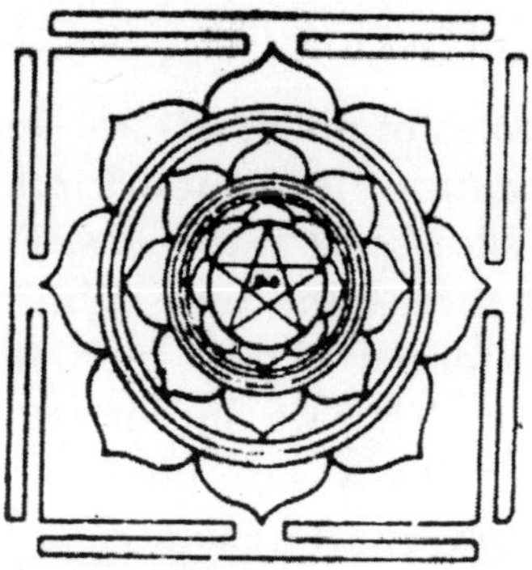

Fig. 11.4 Sri Mahamrtyunjaya Yantra

Refrain

There are refrains of triangles in all the yantras. You can also see the refrains of flower patterns in all yantras. If you closely inspect these yantras you will find the refrains of circles in all of them.

Palindrome

The spatial correlate of the palindrome is mirror symmetry. For example, in Fig. 11.4 if you imagine the central vertical axis to be a mirror, the left side is the image of the right side and *vice versa*. A similar central horizontal axis when treated as a mirror gives a near-symmetry. In all these yantras you will find that the horizontal and vertical axes will almost yield mirror symmetries. In fact with respect to some elements there are many more axes of symmetry. For instance, with respect to the flowers in Fig. 11.3 there are four axes: one horizontal, one vertical and two diagonal. There is another kind of symmetry called rotational symmetry. For example, if the borders of all these yantras are rotated through 90°, 180° and 270° you get back the same border pattern. We will not discuss the rotational symmetry further because it leads to complex analysis.

Multiplets and Cycle

The spatial correlates of multiplets are the symbols which appear in many yantras: the bindu, circles triangles and squares may be called space multiplets. There is however, one difference between the time multiplets and space multiplets. In the former a given multiplet has the same number of elements. Thus we find duos, triads and so on. In the latter the emphasis is on the form rather than the number. For example, Figs.11.2 to 11.4 have two, six and six circles respectively.

There are also standard inscriptions which are verbal multiplets such as *Om, Om namah Shivaya, Bhuh Bhuvah Svah* and so on. These appear as inscriptions on the yantras.

Any closed figure appearing in a yantra may be called a cycle. In the yantras illustrated here you can find a number of cycles.

Embedding

Hanumana yantra is an inverted triangle with a few inscriptions. You will see this yantra (except for inscriptions) embedded in all the yantras illustrated here. Look at the centre of Fig. 11.2. There are three triangles of which two triangles intersect each other. This duo (with some incriptions) itself is a yantra called *Dhana - yasha - prapti* yantra used for acquiring wealth.

Pattern Completion

To understand the role of pattern completion in space consider Fig. 11.3. If you delete the topmost petal, you are bound to feel that the yantra is not complete and something is missing. Reinstate this petal and you have completed the pattern. In fact pattern completion is very closely related to our appreciation of symmetry.

Other Patterns

Other patterns may also be pointed out but sometimes the space-time correspondence becomes tenuous in some cases and less important in others. Overlapping is obvious where two figures interesect Recursion can also be detected but needs considerable effort to identify and express formally. Consider a simple case: a bindu surrounded by many concentric circles. A little introspection will tell you that a bindu to which circles are added progressively exemplifies recursion.

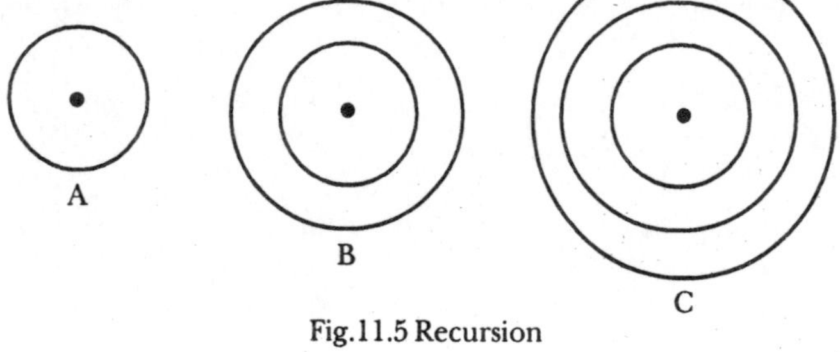

Fig.11.5 Recursion

You can start with "A bindu surrounded by one circle". The recurrence formula is replace *bindu* by *bindu surrounded by a circle.* We get the following successive figures.

A bindu surrounded by a circle (Fig.11.5A)

A bindu surrounded by a circle, surrounded by a circle.(Fig.11.5B)

A bindu surrounded by a circle; surrounded by a circle, surrounded by a circle (Fig.11.5C); you may continue without end.

Tantric geometry, if such words can be used, has many other interesting facets. For example, patterns such as Latin squares containing numerals are used frequently in tantra.

It should not be thought that spatial ritual patterns occur only in tantra. They are also present in other rituals, religious as well as secular though not as abundant as in tantra.

It is interesting to see how one square containing numerals can be obtained from another by such techniques as rotation or interchange of numerals in various columns and rows. Unfortunately the scope of this book does not permit me to elaborate many fascinating structural aspects of rituals.[1]

End Note

[1] You will find some other yantras in Burde (2004) chap.3. The same book discusses structural aspects at length in chap.7.

12

Animal Rituals

Rituals as rhythmic activities are not confined to humans. A brief account of animal rituals especially those found in primates will convince you that rituals are instinctual drives rather than learned behaviour though in case of humans rituals can be designed in a deliberate fashion.

Exploration and Phobia

Those who have extensively studied animal rituals identify two conflicting tendencies giving rise to ritualistic behavior. The first is called *neophilia* (love of the new). This exploratory urge is quite manifest in human babies and young monkeys. The young ones explore the new through manipulation till they are thoroughly familiar with it and then abandon it in favour of a newer unknown territory. Like human children, young chimpanzees are attracted to toys and invent simple games. They try their hand at drawing and redrawing lines creating ritualistic behaviour. There is no other incentive except the pleasure of playing in which rhythm is invariably involved. In order that the exploratory urge does not lead to violence human adults exercise control over children. Adult chimpanzees seem to control their little ones in a similar way.

There is an opposite innate urge called *neophobia* (fear of the new). All of us harbour the fear of the unknown. Monkeys too have such phobia which acts as a check on the overzealous young members. These two opposite urges ultimately decide the type and limitations of ritualistic behaviour.

Music and Dance

Percussion is the most common rhythmic activity found in humans as well as chimpanzees. Exploratory urge leads chimpanzees to experiment with different sounds obtained by banging and striking. Repetition becomes ritualistic in which the whole group of chimpanzees may join. It is not much different from social dancing or clapping found in human groups. It demonstrates an instance of chorus which perhaps has another function: expression of solidarity or social bond with other members of the species.

Music appears in a similar way in the society of chimpanzees.

Hoots, screams and other vocal sounds made by a group of chimpanzees may be called a precursor of what we call music. Primates' cerebral abilities being rather limited, their music remains at the instinctual level, though they may try various combinations propelled by their exploratory urge. Humans, on the other hand, are capable of shaping the rhythmic instinct into an aesthetically appealing music. It must be remembered that nonhumans lack the necessary vocal apparatus, which seriously hampers their progress in music.

If mammals can appreciate percussion and music, they also do a bit of dancing which is closely associated with beats and music. This is especially so in case of primates like chimpanzees who sway and jig while they experiment with drumming, and their mood-indicating quasi-music.

That gymnastics is instinctual can be easily appreciated when we study the behaviour of mammals. As Desmond Morris observes "Rhythmical physical performances are common in the play of both young chimps and young children. They rapidly become stylised, but retain a strong element of variability within the structured patterns they assume. But the physical games of chimpanzees do not grow and mature, they fizzle out..."[1] In case of humans they lead to highly sophisticated games and exercises that may need implements and other paraphernalia used in different sports.

According to Morris such activities as painting, sports, exercise, games etc. are governed by 'play rules'. He has listed six rules that are applicable to infants as well as adults: (1) the unfamiliar is investigated or explored till it becomes familiar; (2) the familiar is repeated; (3) such repetitions are made in all possible ways; (4) the individual or group selects those combinations and variations which yield maximum benefit to the concerned individual or the group at the cost of the adversary or competitor; (5) these variations are "combined and recombined" and (6) these activities and rules themselves constitute a goal, there is no other meaning or motive that can be assigned to them.[2]

Of course, the last rule is subject to some provisos especially in case of humans where games may be played for status or money. However, these benefits are secondary, the primary benefit is instinctual satisfaction of playing and ritualising which involve rhythmic activities leading to a sense of well-being.

Higher animals also display ritualised behaviour that cannot be classified as 'play'. Some engage in ritualised combat in which there are threatening gestures and counter-gestures till one of the adversaries symbolically accepts defeat. We can appreciate this ritualisation if we remember that when two rivals confront each other, each of them is under the influence of two conflicting instincts: attack and flight. This conflict leads to many physiological processes creating metabolic imbalance. It is believed that in the course of evolution these reactions have been ritualised. They appear as a threatening posture and crouching posture: rhythmic shaking usually reflects this termoil.

In primates we often observe complex ritual threats and

'combat dances' in which the adversaries circle around each other. "They may bow, nod, shake, shiver, swing rhythmically from side to side or make repeated stylised runs."[3]

Humans display similar behaviour: clenching of fists, rhythmic gesture of pointing finger or other gesticulations accompanied by facial contortions conveying the message "just wait, I shall show you". We also see crouching, begging or prostrating in which the actor seeks mercy. A ritual like clenching of fists have a goal of intimidating the adversary, in contrast to the play ritual which can be an end itself.

There is a third type of ritual called *displacement activities.* This is found in case of individuals who are socially inactive or isolated. Such individuals, humans as well as primates, are engaged in repetitive activities such a rocking, swaying, pacing, thumb sucking and so on. These displaced activities are always stereotyped and ritualistic.

If you recall your own behaviour when you were under stress or were embarrassed for some reason, you will find that you often deviated from the main activity to a displacement ritual. Playing with our tie, repeated drumming of the table, whistling etc. are some of the rituals we engage in, in order to reduce tension.

Heartbeats

Earlier we remarked that apart from rituals, there are many phenomena where rhythm is present. It has been contended by many researchers that the mother's heartbeats play an important role in the emotional life of the offspring.

It has been found that eighty per cent of mothers cradle their babies in their left arms and hold them against the left side of the chest. It might look natural because the right hand is then free to manipulate the infant. However, further research shows that this has nothing to do with 'left-handedness' or 'right-handedness'. It has been posited that holding the infant against the left chest has the soothing effect on it. The babies feel comfortable if the mother's rhythmic heartbeats are audible to them. It is possible that this is the result of the infant's pre-natal experience. The growing embryo in the womb is imprinted with the rhythm of the mother's heartbeats. Experiments on new-born babies confirm that beats of the same frequency as those of the heart (about 72 per minute) have a soothing effect on the babies. What is more relevant is that between the actual heartbeats and the simulated beats the babies prefer the former. It is also found that the cradling frequency used by mothers to pacify their babies almost equals the heartbeat frequency.

This is not all. We do not forget this rhythmic frequency as we become adults. We react to the heart rhythm in the same way as the infant reacts. This may appear far-fetched but several experiments conducted so far seem to corroborate this theory. When we are under stress we may sway, tap or nod continuously in order to reduce our anxiety. The frequency of the rhythmic activity seems to match that of the heartbeat.

Characteristic Sounds and Faces

Morris tells us that the pre-linguistic sounds babies make are species-specific.[4] In other words when a baby chimpanzee grunts, screams or moans it emits sounds that are common to all chimpanzees. In case of humans, too, such mood-signals emanating from infants are typical and are instinctive, not learnt. When we grow up we use language to communicate with clarity, but we never give up instinctive cries and screams.

While these instinctual sounds appear in all mammals, higher mammals also show 'species-faces'. The characteristic facial contortions act as signals to others, especially parents. We instinctively know from one's face whether the person is in pain or under threat, or is expressing her disgust.

It is necessary to remember that the first sound we expect from the new-born is crying. Laughter and smiling appear in infants much later. What's more, some psychologists distinguish between smiling, laughing and 'laughing at' because they convey different messages from children as well as adults.

To conclude, all rituals we mentioned in this chapter had two important characteristics; they displayed rhythm and they were rooted in instinct.

End Notes

[1] Morris, p.113.
[2] Ibid., p.113.
[3] Ibid., p.126.
[4] Ibid., p.94.

13

Instinct and Culture

We have seen that rhythm is the basis of rituals. We found that rhythm does not have to be learnt, its appreciation is innate and so is our response to rhythm. One may postulate that ritual has instinct as a major component. We may call it *ritual instinct,* which is closely related to rhythm. The fact that higher animals, especially primates, too, engage in ritual activities should strengthen our belief about the instinctual nature of ritual.

If we assume the existence of ritual instinct we have to reconcile the fact that rituals appear in different forms: animal rituals differ from human rituals and even among humans rituals vary from one society to another. It is not difficult to account for these differences. To begin with we may concentrate on human society. It is easy to see that human ritual is the product of two components; ritual instinct which is common to all human beings, and culture which differs to some extent from one society to another. We may retain the concept of ritual instinct and assert that the ritual form as well as content is modified by culture.

Instinct

Ethology is the branch of knowledge which studies animals in natural setting. Instinctive behaviour is the innate or unconditioned predisposition towards behaviour pattern found in all 'equivalent' members of a species. 'Equivalent' roughly means the same class or category such as male vis-a-vis female, infant as against adult and so on. In fact equivalence connotes some classification on the basis of a definite criterion. Instinct is believed to be genetically determined.

Instinctual behaviour can be observed with greater ease in case of birds and many animals because they can be found in natural settings. In case of domesticated animals, the behaviour of the species is modified on account of human influence on them. Since it is virtually impossible to find humans in natural state we have to isolate the instinctual component by comparing different human societies.

In order to study unlearnt behaviour scientists concentrate on those members of the species which have been isolated right from birth. For us bird songs are very important because they display many of the ritual patterns. M.Me Pessel's studies of the isolated canaries confined to sound-proof cages as soon as they were hatched have yielded interesting results. The scientist found that at the appropriate age they all sang the elementary songs which are believed to be characteristic of their species.[1]

However instinctual behaviour can be altered to some extent through training. For example, in the above case if canaries are reared along with other species, some changes in their 'natural' songs can be found. A canary can be trained to whistle a simple tune.

It is also believed that individuals inherit the instinct of the species in different degrees. It should not surprise one if a species contains a few freaks that show no characteristic instinctual behaviour.

In India some abandoned children have been found to have grown up with animals. A case of two children who were found in a den of wolves has been discussed by J.A.L. Singh and R.M. Zingg in their work, *Wolf-children and Feral Man.*[2] According to them the children "walked on all fours, made howls like wolves and wolfed their food and had other reactions similar to wolves".

We know that the behaviour of domesticated animals differs considerably from that of their feral (wild) cousins.

Nature of Instincts

Many instincts have been mentioned in the past: sex, self-preservation, the instinct for hoarding trash, and even death instinct. There are also 'social' instincts such as herd instinct and gregariousness.

An instinct, unfortunately, is not a simple unconditioned reflex, it is a complex of tendencies. Moreover, humans are believed to possess instincts which are weaker than those in animals. Some instincts appear to overlap while some appear doubtful.

Harry Harlow studied monkeys' behaviour over thirty years and came to the conclusion that maternal instinct may be a myth. Since children are often abused by parents, what we call maternal instinct could be the behaviour partly acquired through learning.

Since instincts are difficult to handle, psychologists use other terms to describe human instinctual behaviour. They speak of 'needs and drives'. Some drives arise to meet specific needs; sleep, hunger, thirst, etc. For instance, we spend about one third of our lives in sleep. Guilford lists an interesting need *viz.* the need for exercise and adds that "this is most apparent in growing children who cannot sit still for very long at a time".[3]

We can add something more to this view: physical exercise appears in may rhythmic patterns as in case of a two-month old baby who does vigorous 'cycling' without any learning.

There are also human needs which are less specific and which can often be gratified through different methods. These include sex, maternal drive (which many psychologists regard as innate), love and affection. A characteristic of such needs is that their satisfaction can be handled with greater flexibility. Some needs like sex can be delayed or even denied.

Guilford also mentions some general needs such as the need to avoid fear producing situations, the urge to fight and struggle, exploratory urge and even need for human beauty and play. The last is extremely important for us. Since the drive for play is flexible it appears in different forms among humans and animals, but most plays have rhythmic basis making us believe in the existence of ritual instinct.

Culture

We know that instinct-driven behavior can be altered to some extent by training or learning. In case of humans the scope for modification and diversity is much more because they possess what is called culture.

There are many creatures who form societies. They are said to constitute *bio-social systems* because their social patterns are mostly determined by hereditary factors. Humans alone are believed to posses what is called a *socio-cultural system.* Human behaviour, strictly speaking, is a bio-socio-cultural system because it is also, though to a lesser extent, determined by heredity.

Culture includes everything man has created for thousands of years: language, literature, buildings or structures, painting, sculpture and in fact all kinds of knowledge and its application. The most important feature of culture is that humans can transmit it to the next generation. The latter does not have to start from scratch. Every generation with its creative ability adds to cultural wealth which has been bequeathed by their forebears, with the result that as time progresses humans become culturally richer and richer. Secondly, a great diversity can be observed between different human societies since each society can make its own unique contribution to culture.

In the lower layers of evolution you find considerable bodily differentiation among the members of the same society. For example, in insects we find a greater physical difference between males and females. Again, females may be divided into queens and workers, and their bodily difference is pronounced. For instance, "in Carebra ants the queen is several thousand times larger than the workers".[4] These differences are considerably less in case of mammals. In lower creatures there is specialisation because of structural (physical) difference. For example, the queen's only major function is reproduction and she differs considerably from workers. Such structural differences are minimal in the mammalian society.

In humans the most evolved creatures, we do find specialisation: some people do manual work, some are engaged in intellectual pursuits, some are doctors, some are statisticians, there is a plethora of diverse vocations. However, these specialisations are cultural rather than instinctual manifestations. We also find considerable variations in customs, mores etc. in different human societies. All these are mainly due to cultural difference.

Studies of higher animals, especially primates, show that the ability to learn increases as you go up the evolutionary ladder. You know that primates can be taught to a great extent. However, attempts to teach them acquire language have failed. It is found that primates do possess very rudimentary signal systems but they are usually based on heredity. Their communication system, if they have any, is instictual closely connected with important needs; food, sex and so on.

Recent researches have made some anthropologists believe that higher primates may possess culture which they are able to transmit to the next generation. However, there is no doubt that if they have any culture it must be very very primitive, and even human efforts to train them cannot raise them to a level higher than a human baby of a few months. Unlike humans other animals including primates simply do not have the capacity to learn except very elementary tasks based on their ability to respond to certain signals coming from the trainer.

Interaction between Instinct and Culture

We now briefly discuss how culture can modify instincts. A general remark would be useful. Usually there is a conflict between two or more instincts or a conflict between the drive and social norms, and finally a conflict between two or more social norms. The last is found especially in liberal societies where the individual has options to select between different customs. It is also found in modern life where a person's mobility takes him to different groups having different norms. Generally it is found that a human being can blend the instincts harmoniously even when he faces multiple standards or customs. This is obviously due to his adaptability through learning. Let us consider a few drives and needs regulated by culture.

Hunger and thirst are basic needs but these can be controlled to some extent: We can postpone eating and drinking by a few hours, we can change the type of food we eat. However, total denial of this need would lead to physical and mental deterioration resulting in death.

Consider the need for sex. There are many rules a human being has to follow depending upon the society in which he lives. Some societies do not tolerate premarital or extramarital sex, some may allow premarital but not extramarital relations. Some primitive societies even encourage premarital and promiscuous sex before marriage so that the young should have an opportunity to select their life partners. After the selection, however, they are expected to marry their chosen spouse. Most societies do not permit sex in public. There may be religious or legal constraints. Usually the marriages of minors are not permitted. Depending upon one's religion there are restrictions on a marriage between close relatives. However there seems to be an almost universal ban on marriage between the parent and child, and that among siblings. The word 'incest' is used for such a prohibitated marriage.

Humans are adaptable and sex can be regulated to a large extent. Deviations from norms do occur but such violations are usually carried out clandestinely. What's more, most societies do not consider such acts as crimes unless they are illegal. For example, premarital sex is still considered a taboo in some societies. However, in many subgroups, it is tolerated if minors are not involved, and provided the act is not publicised.

You can see how rituals are shaped by culture if you examine the customs of different societies. In some societies religious rituals are rigid, complex and long. In others they are minimised. In India new religious sects such as Brahmo samaj or Arya samaj were founded to avoid rigidity of rituals and inhuman practices such as untouchability. However, it must be realised that rituals cannot be eliminated from religion. They cannot even be banished from any society, theistic, atheistic, agnostic socialist or communist. Rituals exist and will always exist whether in religion, politics, social intercourse or the military. Only, they appear in different forms in different cultures. In the simple case of greeting, we may shake hands, fold our hands in the form of *namaste,* bow or salute to greet a guest. All these are rituals reflecting the expression of rhythmic instinct modified by culture.

One final remark is necessary. Total denial or substantial restrictions on a need such as food will lead to the frustration of an instinct or a drive. It will result in undesirable consequences depending upon the nature of the instinct, cultural milieu where the person was raised and, of course, the constitution of the individual. The result could be anger, depression and other abnormal behaviour, physical and mental deterioration and even death depending on the configuration of various factors.

To summarise, studies of animal and human behaviour indicate that rituals are manisfestation of instinct in which rhythm plays the most important role. We have called this ritual instinct. While in case of animals this instinct is a major component, in case of human societies the instinct interacts with culture, which explains diversity in ritualistic behaviour.

End Notes

[1] Guilford, p.70.

[2] Published by Harper and Brothers (1942). Cited by Guilford, p.90.

[3] Guilford, pp.99-100.

[4] Davis, Kingsley (2004), p.33.

14

Why We Perform Rituals

The words such as *interpretation* and *meaning* have many connotations. When we speak of a meaning or interpretation of ritual, we are actually answering one or more of the following questions.

1. Does ritual mean what it appears to indicate, or does it have a symbolic significance?
2. Why should we perform ritual? Is there any rationale?
3. Does a ritual have a cause?
4. What is the goal of a ritual, if there is one?
5. Does ritual fit into a grand plan authored by God or Nature in which all of us are mere pawns?
6. Is it necessary that a ritual should have a meaning other than ritual itself?
7. Is it possible for a ritual to have different interpretations all equally valid?

These questions are not mutually exclusive and the answers, too, will appear to overlap. The problem of meaning and interpretation is not confined to rituals. It would be instructive to briefly discuss theories relating to this problem.

Existentialism

Existentialism in general stresses the limitations of rationality. It lays emphasis on feelings and awareness that lead to transrational acts. Edmund Heidegger (1859-1938) is one of the earliest existentialists. According to him, the proper mode of human existence lies in man's responsibility for what he creates. Unlike other creatures humans have greater creative ability through choice. He postulates that this mode is manifest when a person is deeply engaged in the world. This mode is *Desein.* There is, of course, a common ground for various modes of existence, which is called *being.* Man alone is capable of displaying *Desein.* An authentic person according to Heidegger is one who acts on his own and responsibly without the crutches of social conventions. Such acts reveal man's freedom.

However, this very unique freedom which humans have is coupled with anxiety which is rooted in human existence.

According to Sören Kirkgaard (1813-1855) personal experience stands in absolute contradistinction with non-personal experience. Each person is confronted with the dilemma of "being or not being himself."

Since anxiety is built into the very existence of humans, all of us use ritual as a shield against anxiety. Existentialism has a merit of leading to the genesis of ritual in all cases whether normal or what psychologists call abnormal.

Paul Tillich, another existentialist, has tried to analyse anxiety further. According to him there are three types of anxieties, which often overlap. He calls the first type *ontic anxiety* (Gk *on* for 'being'). The greatest dread we have is the dread of death which threatens our existence. Derived from this basic anxiety is the anxiety of fate. At every step we face uncertainty and contingency, and we have to make choices using our freedom. This raises a perpetual anxiety related to 'contingecy'. In the common man's words, this anxiety is: "I don't know what will happen at any moment. I'm frightened because I would not know how to face a situation which arises without foreknowledge".

Tillich relates the second type of anxiety to emptiness and meaninglessness. Humans self-affirm spiritually every moment. They can live spontaneously by creating something new because to a great extent they can manipulate the environment. According to him this self-affirmation is threatened by non-being. The absolute threat of non-being leads to emptiness while a relative threat in a specific situation gives rise to meaninglessness.

The third type of anxiety is the threat to *moral* self-affirmation from non-being. For example, when the judge within us, which we call conscience, may question our actions leading to guilt feelings in specific situations. There may be a general threat in the sense we feel totally rejected by our own inner voice.

Our rituals perform the task of reducing or concealing the existential anxiety as if through diversion.

Sigmund Freud

Sigmund Freud was an Austrian neurologist who founded psychoanalysis. His study of the *unconscious,* which is often called *subconscious,* had a unique approach. He studied the mind by probing the unconscious of patients who showed abnormal behaviour.

Freud used two main tools to understand the patient. First, interpretation of the patient's dreams, and secondly the use of 'free association'. The latter technique was developed by Freud where the patient is asked to relax on a couch and express himself freely without any inhibitions. Freud believed that sooner or later the patient's rigidity is reduced and his speech can be analysed to interpret his mental symptoms. He also developed a theory of interpreting dreams in his famous book *Interpretation of Dreams.* Analysis of a dream was believed to help the psychoanalyst in the same way as the technique of free association.

Freud's psychoanalysis encompasses a personality theory as well as a therapeutic method. Freud recognises three subsystems of our personality; *id,* roughly equivalent to the group of instincts, especially sexual instinct with which we are born; *ego,* approximately equal to what we feel as 'self' and the part which is in touch with reality; *superego,* roughly equivalent to conscience. In a normal person these three subsystems should work in cooperation. Any excessive imbalance or inner conflict would lead to abnormal behaviour.

All of us use what are called ego defences to allay our anxiety and guilt. Clinical psychologists believe that in the abnormal person such defences are excessive to the extent that the person's sense of reality is distorted. We may briefly describe these defences, since they *may* lead to symbolic rituals in some cases.

Denial of reality is a defence which helps most of us to reduce our anxiety. For example, we may postulate that after death we go to heaven to enjoy a better life. Related to this is the defence of *fantasy*: we may day-dream that one day we will be very healthy and rich. Fantasy makes us forget, though temporarily, our ill-health or poverty.

In *rationalisation* we try to justify our anti-social or any incongruent behaviour or our failure through specious logic. *Projection* is a defence in which we attribute to others our own feelings or motives. In *repression* we make our painful experiences or harmful desires unconscious. *Reaction formation* not only shows repression of painful experience, it displays opposite behaviour. This is normally found among the guardians of morality and public preachers.

An important defence is *undoing* or *atonement.* If we feel we have committed a sin, we may try to wipe it off through charity. A person may also indulge in such activities as washing the hands continuously or repeating a magical mantra. *Displacement* is a defence in which our emotions, memories, symbolic meanings etc. undergo a shift so that any trauma becomes less painful. In *Emotional insulation* and *intellectualisation* we try to belittle the gravity of the situation and thus try to reduce our anxiety. Many cynics who pooh-pooh social customs suffer from anxiety which they try to hide by wearing a mask of nonchalance.

Sublimation indicates a person's method of channeling her

instinctual, especially sexual, energy in socially acceptable goals.

All of us use these denfences at one time or another. In religion rituals and mantras may play a role of reducing anxiety. Many rituals can be explained on the basis of these defences. However, there are problems concerning 'interpreting' a ritual correctly. We shall discuss it later.

The importance of Freudian theory lies in the fact that the obsessive compulsive behaviour or OCD which we described earlier is a ritualistic behaviour with a difference:-it is without doubt abnormal and painful to the patient. After Freud introduced psychoanalysis, it was believed that OCD is one of the few mental abnormalities which were amenable to psychoanalysis. For us OCD is also important because it is a bridge between the normal ritual and pathological ritual.

While Freudian theory seems to offer a plausible explanation of abnormal behaviour in which various defences mentioned above are deployed to reduce or shield anxiety, its application is patient-specific. The symptoms are 'interpreted' by the analyst and hence to some extent the therapeutic road is centered around the patient-therapist relationship. There are many difficulties in such interpretations which will be briefly discussed in a later chapter.

Transactional Analysis (TA)

Transactional Analysis provides many insights into the genesis of rituals, especially social rituals.

Transactional Analysis was founded by Eric Berne a Canadian psychiatrist who moved to the U.S. where he studied psychoanalysis. It "is based on the observation that all of us are three persons in one".[1]

In a way each of us has three actors living together in our mind: Child, representing our childhood experiences with a large instictive portion, Parent or parents as we saw them, symbolising authority, and Adult, our rational self which has a greater rapport with the real world.

According to this theory an infant has 'stimulus hunger' which can be satiated through petting, hugging and coddling by elders. Later, the stimulus hunger is transformed into *recognition hunger,* the desire to be recognised as a separate individual. If you attend a function where you are ignored by the very person who invited you, you are likely to be hurt because your presence was not noticed. On the other hand, if you are greeted with a smile, you are likely to be elated and feel important.

The stimulus hunger and recognition hunger are said to be satisfied when the child is petted or someone acknowledges even by a simple gesture, the child's presence. The technical term for the social transaction which satisfies these hungers is 'stroke'; a stroke is a fundamental unit of social action. It is truly believed that an infant who receives no stroke is more unfortunate than the one who receives a negative stroke, say, scolding.

Next in the hierarchy of hunger comes the *structure hunger.* This relates to the problem of how we structure our time when we are not asleep. Eric Berne maintains that all social living in cooperative aspects addresses this problem.[2] If the stimulus hunger and recognition hunger is not satiated, sensory and emotional starvation will follow. Structure hunger if not attended to can lead to boredom. In the extreme case of 'no strokes', biological deterioration is bound to occur.

Complementary Transactions

When two or more people meet, one of them may start conversation or make some gesture to which the listeners will react in different ways. To simplify matters, suppose there are only two adults who meet each other. The person who starts conversation creates what is called the *transactional stimulus.* The other person's reaction is the *transactional response.* These transactions are called complementary if we feel that the response is appropriate, expected and within the territory of the prevailing custom.

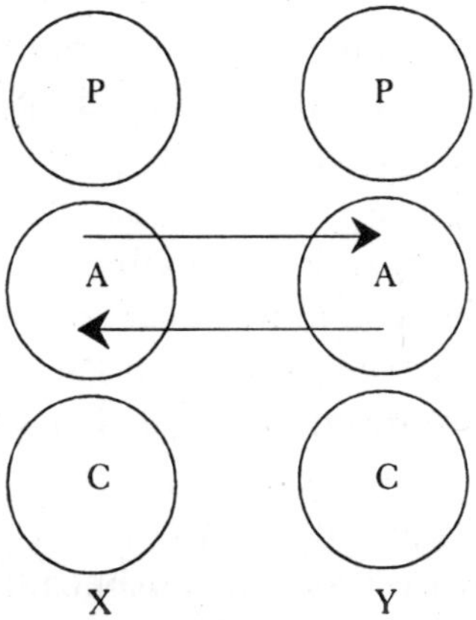

Fig. 14.1 Complementary Transaction

In Fig. 14.1 we have shown two persons X, Y involved in transaction. Transactional analysts use three circles to denote the Parent (P), Adult (A) and Child (C) within each person. Consider the following conversation:

X: Hi, How are you?

Y: Very well, thank you. How's your business?

X: Fine, OK see you later, I am in a hurry.

This transaction is quite simple and on expected lines. In the conversation Adults of both X and Y are involved. The stimulus (X to Y) evokes an appropriate response (Y to X). Not only X and Y but even an onlooker is bound to feel that the conversation is complementary.

To be brief, ritual according to transactional analysis is 'a stereotyped' series of simple complementary transactions programmed by external social forces. It is easy to see that a ritual form is parents' legacy *i.e.*, Parentally determined by tradition.

If you recall what we said earlier, in complementary transactions or rituals the persons involved are giving and receiving expected strokes. Earlier we saw a peculiar reaction to the stimulus 'hello'; the friendly *hello* was greeted with a blow on the head of the person who initiated the transaction. In such cases transactions are not complementary and the ritual is broken. So long as complementary transactions continue the communication is smooth and ritualistic.

However, this simple illustration in Fig. 14.1 is not the only type of complementary transactions. For example, suppose you meet an older acquaintance who is fatherly and has often guided you in the past. Your conversation may be similar to that between the good Parent and the happy Child. In this case the transaction is between Parent (your acquaintance) and Child (you). These transactions constitute a ritual. But suppose your acquaintance remembers an incident in which he was injured because of a mischief you played fifteen years ago. His face suddenly becomes threatening and he blurts out: "I will never forgive you for what you did to me. I will settle the score some day". He has ceased to be a good Parent. In fact his Child has taken over and the ritual breaks down.

Transaction analysists use many other types of transactions such as 'procedure', 'pastime', 'game' etc. which we need not consider at length. For example, in a game the actors usually have ulterior motives and the apparent transactions have a different level than the hidden transactions. However, even a game when played frequently, according to the 'rules of the game' in which each actor is allowed to be a hypocrite to a certain extent becomes stereotyped and may be called a ritual which has two different levels; one is the 'ostensible', having semblance of complementary rituals and the other is the 'hidden' which constitutes a game.

When rituals are vitiated for some reasons they are said to be contaminated. However, many rituals which have been contaminated have been transmitted from one generation to the next. After many generations these contaminated rituals become a matter of faith. They may not reflect the customs and intent which the forbears of this generation contemplated. It is only faith that gives a time honoured ritual its acceptability. As Berne points out "Transactionally they represent guilt relieving or reward seeking compliances with traditional Parental demands. They offer a safe, reassuring (*apotropaic*) and other enjoyable method of structuring time".[3]

We reiterate that for us a ritual is a stylised behaviour which recurs and displays some ritual patterns. We will not use the word ritual in a restricted sense as transaction analysts do.

End Notes

[1] Berne (1968), p.34.
[2] Harris (—), p.10.
[3] Berne (1968), p.34.

15

Interpretation of Rituals

In the last chapter we considered a possible reason for the need of performing rituals. This may be called the general factor – the need to protect one's anxiety. However, individual rituals were not analysed and opinions usually reflected the viewpoints of scholars who are not themselves involved in performance of rituals.

TRADITION

If you ask a priest, a yajamana, or any actor involved in performance of a religious ritual, you are likely to be told that rituals have some goals such as follows:

(1) A religious ritual may have a lofty goal such as maintaining equilibrium of the universe.

(2) Rituals are performed for acquiring wealth, health and happiness. They are performed so that our wishes are fulfilled.

(3) Rituals are performed to have a happy afterlife or for liberation from the cycle of birth and death.

(4) Rituals are performed as a matter of duty or tradition.

(5) Very rarely, a goal is not specified.

In (1) to (3) the ritualist obviously believes in magic or in God who will reward him. In (1) he is trying to allay anxiety *viz.* the universe may fall apart leading to his own annihilation.

As far as (4) is concerned, we must remember that the force of tradition is much stronger than we usually estimate. This can be gauged from the fact that while laws have been created or amended to eliminate unhealthy practices and superstitions, customs have proved stronger than progressive legislation. For example, in India persecution of the scheduled castes still prevails, daughters are still considered liabilities and the practice of *saṭi* or burning oneself after the death of one's husband and human sacrifices are not totally extinct.

Western Scholars

Western scholars, too, have offered several explanations of ritual.

(1) Rituals mirror myths and symbolise their enactment.

(2) Rituals reflect social milieu.

(3) Rituals are used to transmit socio-cultural values especially in preliterate societies.

These explanations are general and to some extent valid. However, many critics have expressed reservations on these views. Staal has raised pertinent questions which these views cannot fully answer.

(1) Why should myths be reenacted? And that, too, through obscure (symbolic) rituals?

This argument loses some strength because ritualisation involves repetition and thus its gist can be retained in memory with ease. Second, there are some taboos such as sex which cannot be discussed freely. Their symbolic representations through ritual is a less embarrassing mode of communication.

(2) It is true that rituals reflect social milieu, but the hypothesis that ritualisation is necessary for transmission of socio-cultural values is not tenable. First, ritualisation occurs also in literate societies. Second, even in preliterate societies such things as myths, legends and ideas about gods and worship are transmitted in ordinary language from parents and grand-parents to the growing generation. According to Staal the only cultural transmission is the transmission of the rituals themselves.

Meaningless Rituals

Staal, however, has taken an extreme step and made a bold hypothesis: ritual has no meaning, goal or aim. It constitutes its own aim or goal.[1] It must, however, be emphasised that for Staal 'ritual' means shrauta ritual which he has studied extensively. Nevertheless, his theory is important for us because it enables us to think of various types of rituals as a continuum with varying degrees of rigidity and meaning. In support of his contention we can furnish the following evidence.[2]

(1) Ritual is not an ordinary activity. In our normal activities the goal is important. If there are different routes to the goal, we choose the one which suits us most. A ritual on the other hand has to be performed exactly in the way prescribed; what is of importance is *orthopraxy* or 'right action'.

(2) There is considerable resemblance between games and rituals. The rules of the game are *constitutive*, that is, they are the meaning as well as the goal. In fact ritual is a better example than games, of this type of activity: in a game you may win or lose; in ritual you are always the winner when you strictly follow the rules. 'Winning' here means performing rituals as prescribed.

(3) The Vedic mantras which should be treated as part of rituals were transmitted without any change. Though sometimes they resemble language, they radically differ from language in that they do not undergo changes as the language does over a long period of time. When a text is translated into another language there is translation of phrases. However, when mantras are exported, they are transliterated and not translated. For example, *Namo Buddhaya* and *Shivaya namah* are not translated as 'Hail to Buddha' or 'Hail to Shiva', but their original form is retained with some adaptations in pronunciation.

(4) Some mantras especially bijas and stobhas appear

meaningless. Some like Purusha Sukta appear out of context in the ritual acts such as *Shodashopachara puja* consisting of sixteen steps.

Animals, too, engage in ritulas. They do 'acrobatics', sway and dance. Morris has called them *play rituals* which are an end in themselves.

(5) A ritual can be interpreted in many different ways; some of them even diametrically opposite to others. These explanations are nothing but *post facto* interpretations calculated to fit in the data in a neat way.

(6) The very assumption that every ritual should have meaning is wrong. We do not point out at a tiger to a zookeeper and ask him "what is the meaning of this?"

(7) One often finds the same rites used in different ceremonies. This necessitates ascription of different meanings to the same rite.

(8) The priest who performs rituals sometimes does not know the meaning of the rituals; he only knows the exact method and follows it because he feels bound to adhere to tradition.

(9) If a ritual had a symbolic meaning it could have been conveyed in a simple language and not in a roundabout fashion.

Hermeneutics

I have listed in the last chapter seven questions relating to the meaning of the very words 'meaning' and 'interpretation'. These words do not convey only one connotation, but has many meanings. This shows the first difficulty in interpreting a ritual. There is another difficulty which pertains to the technique of interpretation. It is usually believed that there exists a science of interpretation called *hermeneutics.* It first appeared in the Hellenic period. This science has two main features: (1) the objective side which relates to the grammatical meanings and their historical variation and (2) the subjective aspect which concerns the interprter's attempt to understand the mind of the author.

In the nineteenth century emerged 'free hermeneutics' which could interpret any situation pertaining to different disciplines: aesthetics, social science, literature and even what we call hard sciences

Fredrich Sheirmercher developed a theory of 'general hermeneutics'. Some of the notable contributors to the theory of hermeneutics are Wilhelm Dilthy, (1833-1911) and his follower E.D. Hirsch, Edmund Heidegger, (1859-1938), H.G. Gadamer and many others. Since in hermeneutics subjective approach to interpretation is always involved it is no surprise that the second difficulty of interpretation is almost insurmountable.

A literary piece can be interpreted in hundreds of ways and will be reinterpreted by every succeeding generation. Similar difficulty arises in Freud's method of dream interpretation or interpretation of neurotic symptoms. A painting and a musical piece can have scores of interpretations depending upon the mental make-up of the experts who interprete them.

I have explained elsewhere at length why hermeneutics cannot be a science.[3] Here I shall provide only one illustration of interpretation.

On a certain day a particular stock index at an Indian stock exchange comes down by 5%. Here are a few interpretations by experts.

(1) A seasoned broker – In the history of the stock market, such falls have occurred periodically about once in three months. This is just a statistical fluctuation and warrants no particular explanation.

(2) An economist – During the last one year there has been 1% increase in the average rate of interest on bank deposits. It is believed that interest rates on deposit will escalate further making stocks less attractive. I attribute the fall of index to the rumors that the central bank (the Reserve Bank

of India) will increase the bank rate soon. I expect that the current downward trend in stocks will continue for at lest two weeks. Investors can enter the market, but should be selective.

(3) An investment consultant – Five huge equity issues are open in the market. Money is being diverted to these issues, since all the offers appear to be lucrative. The secondary market will be down for another sixty days. Be cautious and base your decisions on the analysis of specific stocks.

(4) A technical analyst – The sudden fall does not surprise me. My charts clearly show the downward trend. Be selective in choosing your scrips.

(5) A statistician – Five top companies with heavy weights in the computation of index have shown significant drop in the market price.

(6) An astrologer – The planetary position for the bourse is not good. I think at least for a week pessimism will prevail in the market.

(7) A politician – A superpower made threatening noises last week against its neighbour. Investors expect an impending attack by the superpower. This anxiety is reflected in the drop of index.

(8) An investor – Why should anyone be surprised? Stock indices in five major exchanges in the world have slumped. This is the effect of globalisation. One has to be cautious and selective.

Different causes are attributed to the index fall. We do not know whether the various assessments are correct or not. On the previous day nobody predicted a sudden fall in the index.

Most interpretations in social sciences are *post facto* rationalisations. You may choose the explanation that suits your temperament. What's more, some of the explanations are spurious like the statistician's comments in (5) above. You will also notice that the various experts, when they make any prediction, about the market movement also ask you to be cautious and selective. Whether you are cautious or selective is decided *post facto*: if you earn a profit, you have chosen the right shares and exercised caution, if you lose, you have been hasty and imprudent. In any case you may win or lose, but the expert is always the winner.

What is true about interpretations pertaining to stock movement is also true in many such cases: interpretation of obscure rituals, dream analysis, historical interpretations and the interpretations of many social phenomena that have occured in the past.

Barring a few interpretations which agree with predictions and where experts as well as lay persons agree almost unanimously, all *post facto* interpretations conflicting with one another should be taken with a pinch of salt.

End Notes

[1] Staal (1983), p.131.

[2] Staal's arguments will be found in detail in his, *Ritual and Mantras* chapter 13.

[3] Burde (2004), chapter 6.

16

What are Rituals then?

What then are rituals? Is it possible to present a paradigm, a comprehensive theory or a model based on rhythm or ritual instinct? Before we make an attempt to formulate a comprehensive model, it is necessary to briefly deal with a few topics not considered so far but which need to be incorporated to complete the understanding of rituals.

Prelinguistic Sounds

Animals utter many sounds which are mood signals and crude communication signals which may serve several purposes: alerting other members of the 'community' of an impending danger, attracting members of the opposite sex, threatening a rival etc. they may also make several gestures to inform others in proximity about their mood or intention. Usually these sounds or gestures are species-specific.

Even a lay person can identify two structures viz. repetition and refrain in characteristic sounds of animals; mewing, neighing, cackling, bleating, grunting and so forth. In fact such sounds have enriched our languages with onomatopoeic words like roar, caw and mew. We can also occasionally detect palindromes, chorus and relay.

Ornithologists have made extensive studies of 'bird songs'.

Some songs are simple utterances which reveal ritual patterns such as iteration, refrain, palindrome, chorus and possibly relay, even to lay persons. However, some songs have more complex structures. When these songs are broken into components comparable to those of mantras, they, too, display ritual structures in which a component is not a simple note, but a group of notes.[1]

Staal finds a striking resemblance between stobhas which are meaningless phonemes such as ha bu, yo no, phal phal phal phal etc.(which are found in Samaveda), and certain rites and structural units of bird songs.

When ornithologists try to correlate these structures with meaning, the only conclusion they can draw is that in some cases there is a correspondence with utility or function (feeding, courtship etc.) but most cases appear to be meaningless. This shows that bird songs are closer to rituals including mantras than with language. We have already shown that language has a syntax different from that of mantras.

Human Babies

Those who watch closely the behaviour of human infants as they grow, find interesting data that can be correlated with ritual acts and mantras.

Before babies learn to speak they perform instinctive rituals. I have already mentioned that two-month old babies move their hands and legs in a manner which has rightly been described by physicians as 'cycling'.

Before they are able to speak babies make prelingual sounds which at some stage are called babbling.

If you have watched infants uttering various sounds apart from crying you must have noticed that their utterances are of the type

pa pa pa pa
ma ma ma ma
va va va va
am am am am
etc.

Many scholars such as Roman Jakobson and Morris Hall agree that the most natural order of sound production is an opening of the mouth followed by its closure. This explains the genesis of many bijas; am, aam... om etc. and stobhas which appear meaningless. These utterings also resemble some vocal patterns of other animals.

If you carefully listen to a few sounds made by a baby you will find that thcy include

ma ma pa pa aba

baba, baby, ma, ai

and so on. It is no coincidence that they also resemble the names of some objects the baby comes into contact with, in earlier stages. Babies utter these sounds which are meaningless but it is the adults who give these sounds a meaning. Most monosyllabic and bisyllabic names of close relatives have origins in such utterings: ma, mama, mom, mummy for mother in Indo-European languages, *Aba, abba, abbe* for father in Semetic languages.

It may even happen that the same phoneme may give rise to the names of close but different relatives, especially in languages not closely related. Thus *mama* means mother in English, French etc., while it means another close relative, maternal uncle, in some Indian languages.

Some scholars agree with Haeckel's biogenic law: the development of individuals (*ontogeny*) mimics the development of evolution of the species (*phylogeny*). It looks therefore that babies utterings resembling bijas and stobhas are remnants of what our distant ancestors uttered before they acquired language. We thus have a strong evidence to suggest that rituals and mantras antedate language. Staal even suggests that language evolved from mantras. He guesses that the evolution of language took place in three stages.

At the first stage appeared mantras of type I. These are simple meaningless bija mantras such as *hum* and stobhas such as *bham.* At the second stage the mantras consisted of the sequences of the mantras of type I, possibly with some syntactic constraints, such as *habu, habu, ... bham, bham.*

Langauge emerged at the third stage when semantic and additional syntactic constraints were imposed on type II mantras. Staal provides an example: *vacham yaccha* or 'Control your speech'.[2]

Thus according to Staal mantras not only antedate language they are its source. Staal sums up his conclusions as follows: Ritual originated when the compound activity of doing things and making sounds grew into a system. This appeared early after the emergence of the phylum chordata. Language was born when that system was used to express meaning probably late in the evolution of *homo sapiens.*[3]

Ritual Science

The word science when used in a broad sense connotes more than hard sciences such as physics or chemistry. It includes such branches of knowledge as social sciences and linguistics. In ancient India there was a science of linguistics as well as rituals. While western scholars have now accepted linguistics as science, ritual science is still struggling for formal recognition.

To be called 'science' a body of knowledge should have the following characteristics: empirical adequacy, abstraction, consistency, provisional nature and generalisation.[4]

Empirical adequacy implies that a scientific theory is verified experimentally. Apart from confirmation of the past experiments, a scientific theory should also be able to predict the results under given data. Abstraction is facilitated through introduction of parameters. In some cases we do not know the exact existential status of a parameter. For example, we know what an electron does, but we cannot claim to know the exact nature of an electron. Electromagnetic radiation in physics and the superego in psychoanalysis exemplify abstraction. It is futile to pursue the ultimate reality of such entities as electron, proton, quantum etc.

By *consistency* we mean that any mathematical tool used in a scientific theory should not lead to contradictions.

All scientific theories are provisional and may be superseded by a refined theory. Such progressive refinements tend to reduce the apparent deviations from the predicted results. For example, Newton's theory has been replaced by Einstein's theory of relativity.

Generalisation implies integration and/or unification of the related theories where usually the number of parameters is reduced. For example, Galileo's physics describes the motion of falling bodies under earth's gravitational force, while Keplar's laws describe planetary motions. Newton's gravitational theory is a unified theory inasmuch as it can explain both these theories.

Staal has discussed at length how the Indian texts relating to rituals constitute a ritual science. In *Rituals, Mantras and Science: An Integral Perspective,* I have shown that ritual science can be built even when the scope of ritual is widened to include any type of stylised and recurring behaviour.[5]

Pathological Rituals

Of pathological rituals mentioned in chapter 4 compulsive rituals are most interesting. First, they display almost all ritual patterns. Secondly, they can be even more rigid than those religious rituals performed by an extremely orthodox worshipper.

Third, the rituals are performed against the wishes of the ritualist himself. There is a compulsion from within. There seems to be a split in which the ritualist's one part becomes harsh and compels his rational part to follow a ritual;. Finally, the obsessional may perform the ritual but the relief is only temporary. Back comes the slave driver and asks him to perform another ritual. Clinical psychologists usually identify this harsh part with the strict superego (conscience) or severe Parent inside.

The conclusion we can draw is that the ritualist is sick and needs medical help. The rituals involve a pathology inasmuch as unlike other types of rituals, they cannot allay the underlying anxiety; the degree of anxiety is abnormally high.

Psychoanalysis

We mentioned in the last chapter that clinical psychologists and psychoanalysts try to interpret individuals' dreams and neurotic symptoms. It is impossible to discuss Freud's theory relating to dreams and neurosis even briefly here. However, a few hurdles may be mentioned.

According to Freud dreams appear bizarre to us because latent thoughts are distorted on account of a few factors. First, the material which appears objectionable to our conscience is censored in several ways. Second, a dream is symbolic of latent contents. Third, the dream uses a process of *condensation.* It is believed that the patient through free association sooner or later will come out with clues to help the analyst to correctly interpret the dream. The analyst also tries to interpret neurotic symptoms in a similar manner.

You will find a similarity between hermeneutics and Freudian technique. At every stage of decoding the dream or pathological rituals there are several interpretations. A symbol may be construed in several ways. The process of 'decensoring' or retrieving the repressed material may lead to several options. Some patients do not reach the stage of 'free association' or to use the technical language they offer (unconscious) resistance. Finally, the analyst is the sole judge to decide what is the interpretation of a dream or ritual. The criticism levelled against this procedure by W.H.R. Rivers is quite pertinent. "Such a method", writes Rivers, "would reduce any other science to absurdity".[6]

Rivers has shown how Freud uses sophistical arguments to explain an ambiguity in the interpretation of one of his patient's dreams.[7]

NEUROPSYCHIATRY

Recent advances in neurosciences have enabled psychiatrists to approach abnormal behaviour in a novel way.

There are many methods of imaging the brain. The most important methods are *photon emission tomography* (PET), and *single photon emmision computerised tomography* (SPECT). These methods reveal any metabolic abnormality in the brain systems. Unlike the syntactic/semantic analysis of a given ritual, such scanning is calculated to reveal abnormalities in the brain. Of course, the concerned neuropsychiatrist assumes that there is a correspondence between a brain state and psychological state.

The systems which participate in pathological rituals involve the following parts of the brain.[8]

Orbital cortex is the underside of the front part of the brain. This part is believed to tell us what we should approach and what we should avoid. Emotions and thoughts are believed to come together here.

Cortex is the outermost layer of the brain. The frontal cortex helps us in advanced and abstract thinking.

Striatum lies deep inside the brain almost at its centre. It has two parts, *putamen* and *caudate nucleus.* The former facilitates the automatic transmission from the sensory–motor cortex of the brain which controls physical movements. The latter performs similar automatic transmission and filtering from the part that controls thoughts.

Basal Ganglia may be regarded as *striatum* for our purpose.

Cingulate Gyrus is at the center, deep inside the brain. This part can give you the signal of dread or severe anxiety.

Thalmus processes the sensory information of your body and does the relay work.

The brain scanning shows that the orbital cortex of the OCD ritualists is overheated or hypermetabolic and the caudate nucleus does not function as the 'automatic transmission station'. It is 'stuck': the patient cannot shift from one behaviour to another behaviour. He is obsessed with one subject or continues certain behaviour repeatedly. But you must remember that these obsessions and compulsions are quite conscious.

In Tourett's syndrome (TS) there are sudden tics and vocalisations which appear as rituals but are involuntary. In TS it is the connection between the putamen and motor cortex that is malfunctioning. According to Amen "TS runs in families and may be associated with several genetic abnormalities in the dopamine family of genes".[9]

Although TS differs from OCD in that the former does not involve conscious compuslions both these maladies seem to be genetically related.

The cingulate gyrus, too, has a role to play in OCD. If it is tightly locked to the orbital cortex, it generates dread and the person feels that a catastrophy will happen if rituals are not performed.

It is interesting to see how evolution is involved in these brain systems. According to Schwartz, the automatic behaviour was hard wired into the brain circuit of our ancstors. In all likelihood these behaviours had to do with avoiding contamination and checking to make sure that they were safe–hat the cave was neither dirty nor dangerous, for example.[10]

In case of human beings the failure of automatic transmission system has atavistic effects–compulsive rituals and obsessions. The person with OCD cannot dislodge intrusive thought. This is often expressed as "the circuit from the orbital cortex, the brain's early warning system is firing inappropriately."

The caudate nucleus is not able to do its functions of modulation and filtering. It is worth mentioning that whenever there is such failure of automatic transmission system, the person may fall back upon the frontal cortex and using conscious thoughts may manipulate his behaviour.

In fact this is the principle used in cognitive biobehavioural therapy to treat OCD.

Thanks to advances in brain chemistry, neuropsychiatrists now realise that in OCD there is marked reduction in the flow of a neurotransmitter called seretonin. A neurotransmitter is a chemical which helps transmit messages from one cell to another. This diminishing of the flow results from the fact that its molecules are deactivated partly by what are called 'reuptake pumps' which are complex molecules. To counter deactivation modern psychiatry uses drugs called SSRI (selective serotonin reuptake inhibitors). Among them are fluoxetine ('Prozac'), fluvoxamine, and clomipramine. Sometimes medication is combined with psychotherapy.

We have devoted much space to pathological rituals because they are unique in that they are performed against the wishes of the ritualist herself. Second, one does not have to 'interpret' rituals as psychoanalysts do. We may say that neuroscientists have learnt much about the brain by studying the images of the malfunctioning of the brain, just as Freud learnt about the unconscious by studying emotionally disturbed patients.[11]

Religious Ritual and Pathological Ritual

In terms of rigidity religious and pathological rituals appear to be in the same category. A person who performs religious rituals harbours great anxiety but he knows the source of anxiety–the feeling that he may not be able to complete the rituals according the ritual manual.

Like the OCD ritualist the religious ritualist also has many taboos which can be attributed to religious orthodoxy. Like his OCD counterpart he observes expiation rites or self-punishment for making errors even inadvertently. Many clinical psychologists and psychoanalysts tend to bracket these two rituals and may use the same idiom to describe the behaviour of the corresponding ritualists.

Nevertheless there are a few differences. First, there is a sense of compulsion in case of OCD; the ego seems to fight his own harsh conscience. A religious ritualist may feel the ritual as a burden, but has made peace with the religious manuals or tradition. He obeys the orders of his conscience and is relieved when the ritual is complete. He has done his duty.

Another difference between these ritual types is that the compulsive ritualist may often switch over from one ritual to another. He may realise that his rituals have no goal unlike his religious cousin who may tell you the ostensible purpose of performing a ritual or that it is a tradition he cannot break.

I am not aware if neuroscientists have made comparative studies of these two types using the technique of brain imaging. Such studies would certainly shed more light on why ritual instinct or drive becomes insatiable in case of OCD.

End Notes

[1] Staal (1993), p.280. In chapter 23, he has dealt with bird songs and their structural resemblances with mantras at length.

[2] Staal (1993), p.266.

[3] See Staal(1993), p.440.

[4] Staal (1993), chapter 26, Burde(2004), chapter 5.

[5] Staal (1993), chapter 26, Burde (2004), chapter 16.

[6] Webster (1995), p.264.

[7] In Burde (2004), p.101 a brief account of this dream will be found. Also see Webster (1995) p.264.

[8] There is no unanimity on nomenclature relating to the brain parts.

[9] Amen (1998) p.93.

[10] Ibid., p.51.

[11] It must, however, be admitted that neuroscience is still in infancy. The correlation between the frontal cortex and caudate nucleus on the one hand and the cortical motor centre and putamen on the other is well-established. However, there are many puzzles which need to be solved. Extreme lack of concentration is called Attention Deficiency Disorder (ADD) and one would think that it is almost the opposite of OCD. Nevertheless TS is correlated with both ADD and OCD. According to Amen (p.93) another neurotransmitter dopamine, too, plays a role. It is the seretonin-dopamine mix which ultimately decides how the pathology takes shape.

17

The World of Rhythm

We have studied rituals from different angles in the previous chapters. You should have no doubt that rhythm is the basis of rituals. We are now ready to collate the data we have gathered so far and present a consistent and comprehensive picture. You may call it a theory or a model.

We defined the word ritual in a broad sense to connote any stylised and recurring behaviour. Rituals occur in all walks of life; social intercourse religion, law and politics, the military and so on. (chapter 1)

There are two main approaches to ritual studies; syntactic (structural) and the more popular, semantic. In this book we selected the structural approach because the semantic (pertaining to the meaning of rituals) studies are beset with ambiguities, contradictions and uncertainties. (chapters 15, 16)

We found that in general, rituals have about ten or twelve structural patterns, which we called ritual patterns or ritual structures. While repetition, refrain, palindrome, and chorus appear universal, other patterns occur in various degrees depending upon the type of ritual. (chapters 2, 3)

We have shown that verse, music, dance, physical exercise, gymnastics, sports and games and even bird songs share ritual structures. (chapters 7-10). Table 17.1 summarises our findings about ritual patterns in various fields.

Table 17.1 Features of Language and Rituals

Features	Language	Verse	Music	Dance	Sports Gym. etc.	Religious Riuuals	Compulsive Rituals
Repetition	No	Yes	Yes	Yes	Yes	Yes	Yes
Refrain	No	Yes	Yes	Yes	Yes	Yes	Yes
Palindrome	No times	Some- times	Some-	Yes	Yes	Yes	Yes
Embedding/ Self embedding	Yes	Yes	Yes	Yes	Yes	Yes	Yes
Multiplets	Rare	Rare	Yes	Yes	-	Yes	Yes
Relay	No	Some- times	Yes	Yes	Yes	Yes	-
Cycle	No	Rare	Yes	Yes	Yes	Some- times	Yes
Overlapping	No	-	Yes	Yes	Yes	Some- times	Yes
Pattern completion	No	No	Yes	Yes	Yes	Yes	Yes
Chorus	No	Yes	Yes	Yes	Yes	Yes	-
Meaning	Yes	Yes	No	Some- times	-	Some- times	-

Our first major conclusion is that rituals of whatever type are rooted in rhythm since our concept of rhythm is based on what all of us feel about verse, music, percussion and dance. However, rhythm is not always obvious. In those rituals which unfold slowly, those in which rhythmic frequency is low, we do not feel the rhythm, but a closer analysis reveals their rhythmic patterns. There is another way to detect rhythm: if a ritual is speeded up, rhythmic patterns especially repetition and refrain would become more conspicuous. Those experts who are trained to appreciate music and dance can detect even the slow rhythm which we ordinary people cannot perceive.

Studies of human behaviour especially those of babies convince us that rhythm is instinctual. The fact that animals, especially higher animals, too, display ritualistic behaviour convinces us that instinct is a major component of rituals. I called it the *ritual instinct* in my book *Rituals, Mantras and Science: An Integral Perspective* (2004). Alternatively, we could call it the rhythm instinct.

However, in case of human rituals, there is also a component of culture: we find that instinctual behaviour including ritual behaviour changes with social milieu. What's more, rituals can also be designed consciously by humans. In case of animals such variations are minimal, depending on the physical factors like environment. For instance, domesticated animals may behave in a manner slightly different from their feral cousins. (chapter 12)

This leads us to another major conclusion viz. human rituals are the product of ritual instinct and culture with varying degrees of instinctive and cultural components.

Consideration of animal and human rituals, prelinguistic sounds uttered by animals and babies' babbling suggests that mantras originated before language. While there is a strong evidence to conclude that mantras gave rise to language, this question is still unsettled. (chapter 16)

If you inspect Table 17.1 you will find that there is an odd man out viz. language. This should not surprise us: we have already shown that language is not ritual. (chapter 7)

We found that there are many hurdles in 'interpreting' individual rituals. However, most scholars agree that there is a general factor involved in all rituals: there seems little doubt that rituals allay anxiety and give a sense of well-being. (chapters 14-16)

While rituals can be classified on the basis of different criteria, two parameters viz. the degree of meaning and degree of rigidity are most important. We can thus have two scales; meaningless-meaningful, flexible-rigid. The first may be called the *semantic scale* in which 0 is assigned to a totally meaningless rituals and, say, 1 shows the fully meaningful rituals. The second scale may be called the *rigidity scale* where 0 shows the least rigid and 1 indicates the most rigid ritual.

The following figures depict the semantic and rigidity scales. We may assume that both are continuums in which rituals occupy appropriate positions.

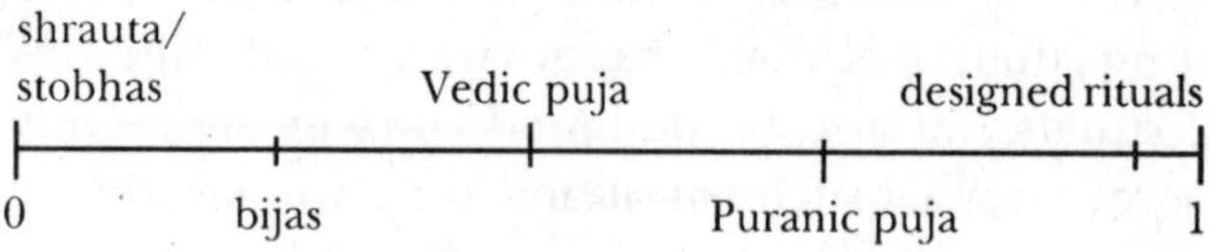

Fig. 17.1 Semantic Scale

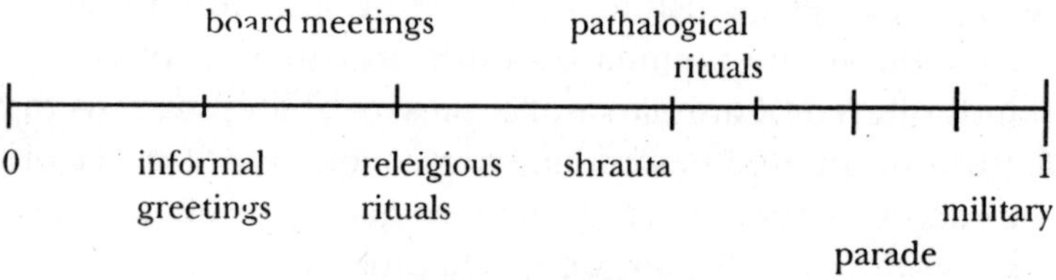

Fig. 17.2 Rigidity Scale

Note that the word *meaningless* is used in a broader sense to indicate those rituals which do not appear to have any meaning or those which can be interpreted in many ways involving ambiguity. A ritual may or may not have any meaning but it will always have rhythm.

Fig. 17.3 shows an interesting graph in two dimensions; semantic (horizontal) and rigidity (vertical):

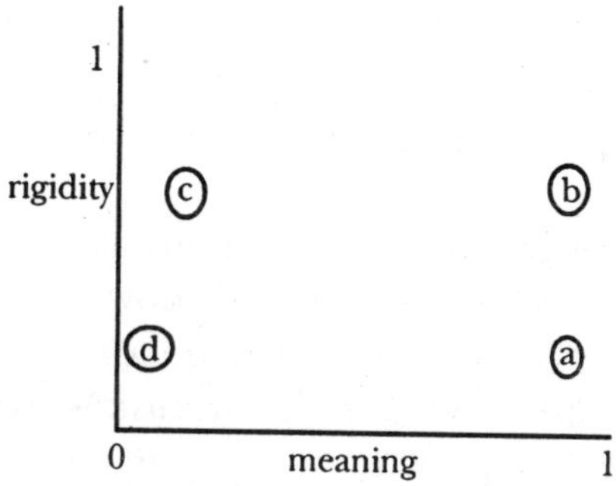

Fig. 17.3 Semantic and Rigidity Features

Actually the region bounded by the axes should be treated as a continuum. Nevertheless for convenience we can identify important regions and the rituals in them.

(a) High meaning and low rigidity: informal greetings.

(b) High meaning and high rigidity: oath taking by legislators.

(c) Low meaning and high rigidity: shrauta rituals, OCD. These are the morphocentric rituals.

(d) Low meaning and low rigidity: those stobhas and bijas uttered in isolation where the pronunciation and timing are not relevant.

A few rituals may be briefly characterised. A ballet may have high meaning and medium rigidity. The *shodasha puja* is a sixteen step worship ritual. Its Vedic version appears a little confusing because with each step a stanza from the *Purushasukta* or the 'Hymn of Man' from the Rigveda is recited. These stanzas appear out place; possibly they were inserted as magiacal elements. In the Puranic version, on the other hand, the puja along with mantras appears to have a high meaning.

Pathological rituals like OCD appear to lack the important characteristic of other rituals, a sense of well-being and reduction of anxiety. We came to the conclusion on the basis of recent findings in neuroscience that it indicates chemical imbalance in some parts of the brain and performance of pathological rituals gives only temporary relief.

As mentioned in the last chapter, there can be a science of rituals. Staal has discussed at length how this is possible. I have myself described how rituals in general can lead to a science and how some types of religious rituals are amenable to general formulation. I had merely conceptualised ritual instinct in the book mentioned earlier. In the present work this concept was amplified and applied to rituals in general; simple or complex, flexible or rigid, meaningless or meaningful, religious or secular. This has led us to the world of rhythm in which rituals appear in the same class as other activities with which we usually associate rhythm; especially verse, music including percussion, and dance.

Bibliography

Abraham, Francis, John Henry Morgan (1985). *Sociological Thought From Compte to Sorokin.* Macmillan, Delhi.

Abraham, M.H. (1993). *A Glossary of Literary Terms.* Prism Books, Bangalore.

Acharya, S.S. (2001). *Rig Veda Vols.I–IV.* Sanskriti Sansthan, Bareli.

(1998). *Sama Veda.* Sanskriti Sansthan, Bareli.

(2001). *Yajur Veda.* Sanskriti Sansthan, Bareli.

(1998). *Atharva Veda Vols.I–II.* Sanskriti Sansthan, Bareli.

Amen, Daniel G. (1998). *Change Your Brain, Change Your Life.* Times Books, N.Y.

Basham, A.L. (2001). *The Wonder That Was India.* Rupa & Co., New Delhi.

Bapat, K.M. (—). *Gorakshanath Yoga.* Raghuvanshi Prakashan, Pune.

Bapat, K.M. (1996). *Svayampurohita.* Raghuvanshi Prakashan, Pune.

Berne, Eric (1968). *Games People Play.* Penguin, Middlesex.

Burde, Jayant (2004). *Rituals, Mantras and Science: An Integral Perspective.* Motilal Banarsidass, Delhi.

(2007) *The Mystique of Om,* New Age Books, New Delhi.

Capra, Fritjof (1983). *The Turning Point.* Flamingo, London.

(1991). *The Tao Of Physics.* Flamingo, London.

Chakravarti, Mohan (2000). *Indrajal.* Kshirasagar and Co., Pune.

Chidbhavananda, Swami (1965). *The Bhagvad Gita.* Sri Ramakrishna Tapovanan, Tirupparaitturai.

Chopra, Deepak (1993). *Ageless Body, Timeless Mind.* Harmony Books, N.Y.

(1990). *Quautum Healing.* Bantam Books. N.Y.

Desai, C.G. (2002). *Gayatri Mantra Sadhana.* Manorama Prakashan, Mumbai.

Deussen, Paul (1980). *Sixty Upanishads of the Veda, Vol.II.* Motilal Banarsidass, Delhi.

Devis, Kingsley (2004), *Human Society,* Surjeet Publication, Delhi.

Dondo, Mathurin (1967). *Modern French Course.* Oxford University Press, Calcutta, (London).

Dowson, John (1992), *Hindu Mythology and Religion,* Heritage, New Delhi.

Einstein, Albert (1979). *Ideas and Opinions.* Rupa & Co., Calcutta.

Frazer, James (1993). *The Golden Bough.* Wordsworth Editions, Hertfordshire.

Freud, Sigmund (1960). *A General Introduction to Psycho-analysis.* Washington Square, N.Y.

Frolov, I. (Ed. 1984), *Dictionary of Philosophy,* Progress Publishers, Moscow.

Gajendragadkar, Arvind (1992). *Vadyavadanache Sampurna Guide,* Unmesh Prakashan, Pune.

(1991). *Sangeetashastrache Guide.* Devadatta Prakashan, Pune.

Guilford, J.P. (1964). *General Psychology.* Affiliated East-West, New Delhi (Van Nostrand).

Harris, Amy B., and Thomas A. Harris (—). *Staying OK,* Penguin, Middlesex.

Headington, Christopher (1983). *Illustrated Dictionary Of Musical Terms.* Hamlyn Paperbacks, Middlesex, England.

Hockett, Charles F. (1958). *A Course in Modern Linguistics.* Oxford & IBH, New Delhi.

Longstaff, A. (2002). *Neuroscience.* Viva Books, New Delhi.

Morris, Desmond (1984). *The Naked Ape.* Laurel, N.Y.

(1994). *The Human Zoo.* Vintage, London.

O' Flaherty, Wendy Doniger (2000). *The Rig Veda.* Penguin, New Delhi.

Phadake, V.K. (1993). *Devapuja Kashi Karavi.* Anjali Publishing House, Pune.

Sahai, Krishna, (2003), *The Story of a Dance,* Indialog Publications, New Delhi.

Sankaracarya (108), Sriyogesvaranandatirtha (1996). *Mantrasastra.* Keshav Bhikaji Dhavale, Mumbai.

Schwartz, Jeffrey M. (1996). *Brain Lock.* Harper Collins, N.Y.

Staal, Frits (1996). *Ritual and Mantras: Rules Without Meaning.* Motilal Banarsidass, Delhi.

Stern, Paul J. (1966). *The Abnormal Person and His World.* Affiliated East-West, New Delhi.

Svanandasarasvati (—). *Patanjala Yogavidya.* Raghuvanshi Prakashan, Pune.

Swami Ashokananda (1995). *Avadhuta Gita Of Dattatreya.* Sri Ramakrishna Math, Madras.

Tigunait, Pandit Rajmani (1983). *Seven Systems Of Indian Philosophy.* The Himalayan International Institute of Yoga science and philosophy of the U.S.A., Honesdale.

(1996). *The Power of Mantra & The Mystery of Initiation.* The Himalayan International Institute of Yoga science and philosophy of the U.S.A., Honesdale.

(1999). *Tantra Unveiled.* The Himalayan International Institute of Yoga science and philosophy of the U.S.A., Honesdale.

Unmeshanand (1997). *Shastra Ase Sangate Part I.* Vedwani Prakashan, Kolhapur.

(1999). *Shastra Ase Sangate Part II.* Vedwani Prakashan, Kolhapur.

(1997). *Tumche Pourohitya Tumhich Kara, Part I.* Vedwani Prakashan, Kolhapur.

(2000). *Tumche Pourohitya Tumhich Kara, Part II.* Vedwani Prakashan, Kolhapur.

Webster, Rechard (1995). *Why Freud Was Wrong.* Basic Books, New York.

Woodroffe, John (1997). *The Serpent Power.*Ganesha & Co., Madras.

Glossary

A

Aavartanam : In *Bharata Natyam,* the structure of one cycle.

Absolute Music : Pure music without words, pictures, etc.

Actor : A person who performs ritual or an activity.

Adavu : A basic dance step in *Bharata Natyam.*

Adibija : 'First seed', Om.

Adult : The rational part of our mind.

Agnichayana : (*Agni* for 'fire' and *chayana* for 'piling') a Vedic ritual of shrauta type lasting for twelve days.

Aroha-avaroha : Seven ascending and seven decending notes associated with a raga.

Atman : Self, identified with Brahman in Advaita philosophy.

AUM : See OM.

B

Bagalamukhi : A tantric path relating to one of the ten great goddesses; the queen of the forbidden tantra.

Ballet : A dance performance with orchestra. It tells a story without words. It originated in France.

Band : A sizable group of instrumentalists usually with wind instruments.

Bharata : A sage who authored *Natya Shastra,* a famous work on dramaturgy.

Bhuh, bhuvah, svah : 'Earth, sky, heaven' prefixed to Gayatri mantra. Also appears as a multiplet.

Bijamantra : 'Seed mantra' usually monosyllabic but can consist of upto ten syllables. According to tantra, the para bindu whose substance is Supreme Shakti splits into three parts – bindu, nada and bija.

Bola : In Indian percussion, various types of sounds.

Brahma : The creator of the universe Brahma, Vishnu (sustainer) and Shiva (destroyer) constitute the Hindu triad.

Break-and-make : A process by which a subritual gets detached from the original ritual and merges with another ritual over time.

C

Chakra : 'Wheel'. The point where more than three energy channels (nadis) meet. The major chakras are along the spinal cord. Also refers to a yantra and mandala.

Chari : The movement of one foot in *Bharata Natyam.*

Child : In TA, that part of the mind which retains the qualities of a child.

Chord : Simultaneous striking of two or more notes; collectively called a harmonic unit.

Choreography : The art of designing a ballet dance, also the sequence of the dance movements.

Chorus : Simultaneous performance of a ritual by several actors.

Cycle : A ritual pattern in which the ritual ends at the point where it starts from. In music and dance, it also means the pattern which recurs.

E

Ego defence : One of the manipulations by the ego under threat, used to minimise the damaging impact.

Embedding : A ritual pattern in which a ritual is embedded in a longer ritual.

Ethology : The branch of knowledge which studies animals in natural setting.

Existentialism : Any philosophy in which existence especially human existence is considered central.

G

Game : In TA, a series of transactions having double meaning. At the visible level transactions appear complementary; but at the hidden level the actors are 'playing a game', their conversation implies something else.

Ganesha : Elephant-headed god. Also called Gajanana, Gaja-vadana, Kari-mukha, Heramba ('boastful'), Lamba-karna (long-eared), Lambodara (pendant-

		bellied), Dri-deha (double bodied), Vighna-harta (remover of obstacles).
Gayatri	:	A most sacred mantra in the Rigveda addressed to the sun. Personified as goddess Savitri. Also a Vedic meter.
Guru	:	Spiritual teacher.

H

Harmony	:	The art of creating chords with a pleasing sequence, used in western music. See *chord.*
Hermeneutics	:	The 'science' of interpretation.
Hridaya	:	'Heart'. In tantra it means that aspect of mantra which is to be visualised, synchronised or 'deposited' on the heart centre. Also a sadhana involving recitation of mantras, which enables the worshipper to identify himself with the power of mantra.

I

Iteration	:	See *repetition.*

J

Japa	:	Repetition of a mantra.
Jati	:	In Carnatic music, a rhythmic pattern.

K

Kampana	:	'Vibration' Continuation of a note without repeating the consonant. For example maa...
Kathak	:	A classical Indian dance, originated in North India.
Kathakali	:	A dance style from the Indian state of Kerala.
Kuchipudi	:	A classical dance, originated in the Indian State of Andhra.

L

Latin square	:	An arrangement of numbers in a square array in which no number appears twice in a row or a column. The total of the numbers in any row or column is the same. Instead of numbers letters are also sometimes used.

Laya : Speed or tempo in Indian music.

M

Manipuri : A classical Indian style of dancing found in North-East India.

Matra : The interval between two beats.

Minuet : A European court dance of 17th century in triple time. In classical symphony its structure is a palindrome.

Mirror : See *palindrome.*

Mohini Attam : A classical dance style from Kerala, a sounthern State of India.

Multiplet : A group of ritual elements appearing in different rituals; 'singleton', duos, trios, etc.

N

Nada : Divine sound. See also *bijamantra.*

Nataraja : Lord Shiva as the dancer.

Natya : In *Bharata Natyam,* dance with three features *nritta, nritya* and enactment (*abhinaya*).

Neophilia : Love of the new.

Neophobia : Fear of the new.

Nritta : In *Bharata Natyam,* pure dance with only rhythm.

Nritya : Dance with rhythm and emotional expression.

Nyasa : A technique according to which the elements of mantras are 'deposited' on different parts of the body.

O

Octave : In western music a scale of seven notes.

Om (Aum) : Pranava, primordial sound also called adibija, Udgitha; identified with Brahman.

Opera : Literally it means 'works'. It is a theatrical play in which actors sing rather than speak. Originated in Italy in 17th century, it is accompanied by orchestra.

Overlapping : A ritual pattern in which successive ritual elements overlap.

P

Palindrome	:	A sentence or a ritual sequence which has the same stucture from the beginning to the end as from the end to the beginning. Also called *mirror.*
Patanjali (2nd century BCE)	:	The author of the *Yoga Sutras* and the founder of Yoga philosophy.
Pattern completion	:	A ritual structure in which the actor completes an already known pattern when he feels that a given pattern is 'not complete'.
Percussion	:	The playing of a musical instrument in which it is struck or its parts are struck together.
Peshkara	:	From *pesh karna* 'to present' or 'demonstrate'. These are introductory pieces before the main theme in an exclusive tabla performance.
Pitch	:	The frequency of a note.
Prana	:	Life-force having modification; also the first modification which controls the breath. Also a name of the active Cosmic Soul.
Puranas	:	'Old'. Legends and stories of olden days. Usually, related to gods, Creation, patriarchs, etc.

R

Raga	:	A melodious sequence of notes in Indian music. A raga is subject to some rules.
Rama	:	Incarnation of Vishnu and the hero of *Ramayana.*
Recital	:	A public performance by a single musician or singer usually with an accompaniment.
Refrain	:	A ritual pattern in which a ritual element recurs.
Relay	:	A pattern in which a ritual is performed sequentially by different actors.
Repetition	:	A ritual pattern in which the same elements appear in succession.
Rishi	:	A seer or a sage. The Vedas are believed to have been revealed to them.
Ritual	:	A stylised recurring behaviour. The word is sometimes reserved for a rigid and formal ritual especially in religion.
Ritual instinct	:	Instinct or innate drive which makes animals and humans perform a ritual without being taught.

Ritual patterns : Structures characterising a general ritual. The patterns are shared by verse, music, dance, gymnastics, sports, etc.

Rondo : An extension of a minuet.

S

Samskara : Polishing or shaping a thing, mantras or even human beings to make the object fit for a particular purpose. In case of humans samskaras are almost synonymous with rituals of passage.

Samvadi : In Hindustani music, notes that have frequency in a raga next only to vadi notes. See *vadi*.

Saptaka : In Indian music, a scale of seven notes from *sa* to *ni*.

Semantics : Meaning, if any, of a ritual.

Shiva : A god associated with destruction. A master of dance, he is known as Nataraja, famous for his tandava dance.

Sol-fa : The set of notations *doh, ray, mi*...corresponding to the notes in the major scale. Also, the system of such notations.

Sonata : In western music, an instrumental piece with four movements.

Sri Chakra : The chakra of the Divine Mother, also called Sri Yantra.

Sri Yantra : See *Sri Chakra*.

Staff notation : The most popular notation used in western music. It consists of a set of five horizontal lines in which the musical symbols are written.

Stobhas : Meaningless mantras such as, ha bu, found in some Vedic rituals.

Syntax : In ritual, the manner in which elements are arranged.

T

Tala : A rhythmic pattern.

Tana : In tana, the notes are sung rapidly with the vowel *a*.

Tandava : Shiva's most famous dance style. Through tandava, Shiva creates, sustains and destroys the world.

U

Upanishads : 'Esoteric doctrine'. Philosophical treatises regarded as part of the Vedas, possibly written in prose interspersed with verse.

V

Vadi : In Hindustani music, notes occurring most frequently.

Vedas : From *vid* 'to know'. Sacred hymns composed between 1500 BCE and 2000 BCE. Of the four Vedas Rig, Yajur, Sama and Atharva, the last seems to have been added later to the first three. The Vedas are considered to be 'revealed' to sages called rishis. Also called *Shruti* or 'what was heard'.

Vyahriti : 'Covering'. The first three vyahritis are *bhuh, bhuvah, svah* usually prefixed to the Gayatri mantra. The other four are *mahah, janah, tapah, satyam.*

W

Waltz : A popular western dance in triple time.

Y

Yantra : 'Device' A geometric figure usually with inscriptions, used in worship especially in tantra.

Index